Power and International Relations

Essays in Honour of Coral Bell

Edited by Desmond Ball and Sheryn Lee

Power and International Relations

Essays in Honour of Coral Bell

Edited by Desmond Ball and Sheryn Lee

Australian
National
University

PRESS

ANU
PRESS

Published by ANU Press
The Australian National University
Canberra ACT 0200, Australia
Email: anupress@anu.edu.au
This title is also available online at http://press.anu.edu.au

National Library of Australia Cataloguing-in-Publication entry

Title: Power and international relations : essays in honour
                 of Coral Bell / edited by Desmond Ball and Sheryn Lee.

ISBN: 9781925022117 (pbk) 9781925022124 (ebook)

Subjects: Bell, Coral.
                 Bell, Coral--Childhood and youth.
                 Country life--Victoria--Ecklin South.
                 Women college teachers--Australia.
                 Women authors--Australia.
                 International relations--21st century.
                 Festschriften

Other Authors/Contributors:

                 Ball, Desmond, 1947- editor.
                 Lee, Sheryn, editor.

Dewey Number: 327.1

Cover design and layout by ANU Press

Contents

Contributors

Robert Ayson is Professor of Strategic Studies and directs the Centre for Strategic Studies: New Zealand. He has held academic positions with The Australian National University, Massey University and the University of Waikato, and official positions in Wellington with the Foreign Affairs, Defence and Trade Select Committee and the External (now National) Assessments Bureau. He has written books on two of the twentieth century's leading thinkers in strategic studies and international relations, Hedley Bull and Thomas Schelling, and is a frequent media commentator on Asia-Pacific security, nuclear issues and New Zealand and Australian defence policy. Robert is also Honorary Professor at the New Zealand Defence Force Command and Staff College.

Desmond Ball is Emeritus Professor at The Australian National University's Strategic and Defence Studies Centre having been Head of the Centre from 1984 to 1991. Professor Ball is the author of more than 40 books or monographs on technical intelligence subjects, nuclear strategy, Australian defence, and security in the Asia-Pacific region. His publications include *The Boys in Black: The Thahan Phran (Rangers), Thailand's Para-military Border Guards; Burma's Military Secrets: Signals Intelligence (SIGINT) from the Second World War to Civil War and Cyber Warfare, Signals Intelligence in the Post-Cold War Era: Developments in the Asia-Pacific Region; Presumptive Engagement: Australia's Asia-Pacific Security Policy in the 1990s* (with Pauline Kerr), *Breaking the Codes: Australia's KGB Network, 1944-50* (with David Horner); *Death in Balibo, Lies in Canberra* (with Hamish McDonald); and *Australia and Cyber-Warfare* (with Gary Waters and Ian Dudgeon). He has also written articles on issues such as the strategic culture in the Asia-Pacific region and defence acquisition programs in the region. Professor Ball was elected a Fellow of the Academy of Social Sciences of Australia in 1986. He served on the Council of the International Institute for Strategic Studies from 1994 until 2000, and was Co-chair of the Steering Committee of the Council for Security Cooperation in the Asia-Pacific from 2000 until 2002.

Geoffrey Barker is a former foreign affairs and defence correspondent for the *Australian Financial Review*. He has previously been a Visiting Fellow at the Strategic and Defence Studies Centre, The Australian National University. Now semi-retired, he was a European and Washington correspondent for Fairfax and News Ltd. newspapers. From Washington he covered the end of the Cold War and of the Soviet Union, including all of the summit meetings between President Reagan and Premier Gorbachev. He benefitted immensely from Coral Bell's insights into the nature of superpower relations.

Ian Hall is Professor of International Relations at Griffith University, Brisbane, Australia. His books include *The International Thought of Martin Wight* (2006), *Dilemmas of Decline: British Intellectuals and World Politics, 1945–75* (2012) and, as editor, *The Engagement of India: Strategies and Responses* (2014). He has also published in various journals, including *Asian Survey, British Journal of Politics and International Relations, European Journal of International Relations, International Affairs*, and the *Review of International Studies*. His research interests include the intellectual history of International Relations and Indian foreign policy.

Sheryn Lee is a doctoral candidate at the Strategic and Defence Studies Centre, The Australian National University, and a non-resident WSD Handa Fellow at Pacific Forum, Center for Strategic and International Studies (CSIS), Honolulu. She holds an AM in Political Science from the University of Pennsylvania, where she was a Benjamin Franklin Fellow and Mumford Fellow. Previously, she has been a researcher, tutor, and TB Millar scholar at the SDSC, and Robert O'Neill scholar at the International Institute of Strategic Studies-Asia in Singapore. She has previously published in *Asian Security* and *Survival,* and co-edited *Insurgent Intellectual: Essays in Honour of Professor Desmond Ball* (with Brendan Taylor and Nicholas Farrelly).

JDB Miller was Head of the Department of International Relations at The Australian National University from 1962 until 1987. He taught at the University of Sydney from 1946 to 1951 and joined the Department of Government at the London School of Economics in 1952. He was the Foundation Professor of Politics at the University of Leicester from 1955 to 1957 and Dean of Social Sciences from 1960 to 1962. His publications include *Australian Government Politics: An Introductory Survey* (1954), *The Nature of Politics (1962), The Politics of Third World (1966), Survey of Commonwealth Affairs: Problems of Expansion and Attrition (1953-1969)* (1974), *The World of States* (1981), and *Norman Angell and the Futility of War* (1986).

Robert O'Neill AO, Hon D Litt (ANU) is an Emeritus Professor of The Australian National University, and an Emeritus Fellow of All Souls College, Oxford. A leading international specialist on strategic and security studies, O'Neill served as Director of the International Institute for Strategic Studies in London from 1982 to 1987, and then as Chichele Professor of the History of War and Fellow of All Souls College at Oxford University from 1987 to 2001. Earlier in his career, O'Neill was Head of the Strategic and Defence Studies Centre at ANU from 1971 to 1982. He served in the Australian Army from 1955 to 1968, and was mentioned in dispatches for his service in the Vietnam War from 1966 to 1967. Professor O'Neill's extensive record of public service includes appointments as Chairman of Trustees of the Imperial War Museum, Chairman of the Council of the Centre for Defence Studies, King's College, London, Chairman of the Council of the

International Institute for Strategic Studies (IISS), Chairman of the board of the Sir Robert Menzies Centre for Australian Studies in the University of London, and Chairman of the Council of the Australian Strategic Policy Institute. He served as Planning Director and first CEO of the United States Studies Centre, University of Sydney from 2006 to 2007. He was a member of the Board of Directors of the Lowy Institute for International Policy from 2003 to 2012. He was awarded an Honorary Fellowship of the Australian Institute of International Affairs in 2009.

James L Richardson was Professor of Political Science, later Professor of International Relations, at The Australian National University from 1975 to 1998. His first book, *Germany and the Atlantic Alliance: The Interaction of Strategy and Politics* (1966), was written at the Center for International Affairs, Harvard, at a time when strategic studies was still a novelty in the universities. After two years in the Arms Control and Disarmament Research Unit in the British Foreign Office, he taught at the University of Sydney from 1967 until moving to Canberra. His interests included Australian foreign policy, the Cold War and détente, the changing international system after the Cold War, and international relations theory. His books included *Crisis Diplomacy: The Great Powers since the Mid-Nineteenth Century* (1994), *Charting the Post-Cold War Order* (co-edited with Richard Leaver, 1993), and *Contending Liberalisms in World Politics: Ideology and Power* (2001).

Brendan Taylor is Associate Professor and Head of the Strategic and Defence Studies Centre, The Australian National University. He is a specialist on great power strategic relations in the Asia-Pacific, economic sanctions, and Asian security architecture. His publications have featured in such leading academic journals as *International Affairs, Survival, Asian Security, Review of International Studies* and the *Australian Journal of International Affairs*. He is the author of *Sanctions as Grand Strategy*, which was published in the International Institute for Strategic Studies (IISS) *Adelphi* series, as well as *American Sanctions in the Asia Pacific* (2010). He is also the editor of *Australia as an Asia-Pacific Regional Power* (2007), *Insurgent Intellectual: Essays in Honour of Professor Desmond Ball* (2012) and *Bilateralism, Multilateralism and Asia-Pacific Security* (2013).

Meredith Thatcher is the former Publications Manager at The Australian National University's Strategic and Defence Studies Centre. She holds a Master of Arts (Hons) and since leaving ANU has worked for Write Limited, a firm specialising in clear communication. She is an accredited editor and technical writer. Through Write she has consulted with government and corporate clients across a range of sectors, including banking, biosecurity, defence, diplomacy, emergency management, energy, infosecurity, legal, and telecommunications.

Meredith has co-authored a book and edited and indexed numerous titles. Her research interests include cyberwarfare, defence, intelligence, and biometric authentication.

William T Tow is Professor and Head of the Department of International Relations at The Australian National University. He was previously Professor of International Relations at the University of Queensland and at Griffith University, and an Assistant Professor of International Relations at the University of Southern California. He has been a Visiting Fellow at Stanford University, and a Visiting Professor at the Rajaratnam School of International Studies in Singapore. His research interests include alliance politics; US security policy in the Asia-Pacific; security politics in the Asia-Pacific; and Australian security policies.

Michael Wesley is Professor of International Affairs and Director of the School of International, Political and Strategic Studies at The Australian National University. His career has spanned academia, with previous appointments at the University of New South Wales, Griffith University, the University of Hong Kong, Sun Yat-sen University and the University of Sydney; government, where he worked as Assistant Director General for Transnational Issues at the Office of National Assessments; and think tanks, in which he was Executive Director of the Lowy Institute for International Policy and a Non-Resident Senior Fellow at the Brookings Institution. He is a Non-Executive Member of the Senior Leadership Group of the Australian Federal Police, a Director of the Kokoda Foundation, a member of the NSW/ACT State Advisory Council of CEDA, and a Board Member of the Sir Roland Wilson Foundation. His most recent book, *There Goes the Neighbourhood: Australia and the Rise of Asia*, won the 2011 John Button Prize for the best writing on Australian public policy.

Hugh White is Professor of Strategic Studies at the Strategic and Defence Studies Centre of The Australian National University. He has worked on Australian and regional strategic, defence and foreign policy issues since 1980. He has been an intelligence analyst, journalist, ministerial adviser, departmental official, think tanker and academic. In the 1990s he served as International Relations Adviser to Prime Minister Bob Hawke and as Deputy Secretary of Defence for Strategy and Intelligence. His recent publications include *Power Shift: Australia's Future between Washington and Beijing* published as a Quarterly Essay in September 2010, and *The China Choice: Why America Should Share Power*, first published by Black Inc. in 2012. In the 1970s he studied philosophy at Melbourne and Oxford Universities.

Photos

Photo 1: Coral Bell (upper left); Sydney Girls High School, c. 1940.

Source: Coral Bell.

Photo 2: Egypt, visit to the pyramids, on the way to England, 1951.

Source: Coral Bell.

Photo 3: On the way to England, 1951.

Source: Coral Bell.

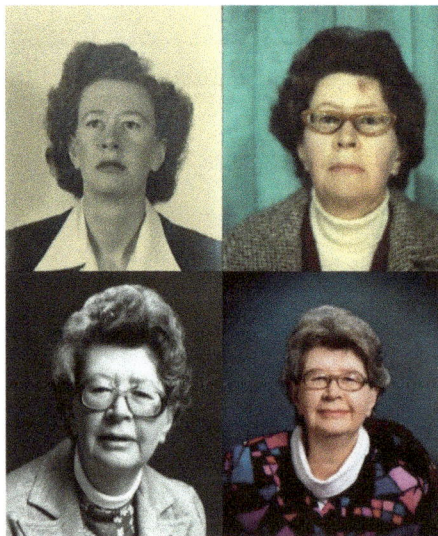

Photo 4: Coral Bell passport photographs.

Source: Coral Bell.

Photo 5: Coral Bell.

Source: Coral Bell.

Photo 6: Coral Bell.

Source: Coral Bell.

Photo 7: The British Committee on the Theory of International Politics, Villa Serbelloni, Bellagio, 27–30 September 1974. Above, from left to right: Kenneth Thompson, Hedley Bull, Maurice Keens-Soper, Robert Wade-Gery, Wolfgang Mommsen (guest); Below, from left to right: Desmond Williams, Adam Watson, Coral Bell, Herbert Butterfield, Max Kohnstamm (guest).

Source: Coral Bell.

Photo 8: Coral Bell, Lowy Institute for International Policy, Sydney, 19 March 2008.

Source: Lowy Institute for International Policy.

Photo 9: Coral Bell, Lowy Institute for International Policy, Sydney, 19 March 2008.

Source: Lowy Institute for International Policy.

Photo 10: Coral Bell and Katherine Morton, The Australian National University, Canberra, 13 July 2006.

Source: Provided by Dr Katherine Morton, Department of International Relations, ANU.

Photo 11: Investiture of Coral Bell's Order of Australia (AO), Government House, Canberra, 2 September 2005. From left to right: Meredith Thatcher, Coral Bell, Brendan Taylor and Betty McFarlane.

Source: Strategic and Defence Studies Centre photo collection.

Introduction

Desmond Ball and Sheryn Lee

Coral Mary Bell AO, one of the world's foremost academic experts on international relations, crisis management and alliance diplomacy, passed away in Canberra on 26 September 2012, aged eighty-nine. She worked at the Royal Institute of International Affairs (Chatham House) in London in the 1950s, was a Senior Lecturer in Government at the University of Sydney in 1961–1965, a Reader in International Relations at the London School of Economics (LSE) in London in 1965–1972, a Professor in International Relations at Sussex University in 1972–1977, a Senior Research Fellow in the Department of International Relations at The Australian National University from 1977 to 1988, and a Visiting Fellow at the Strategic and Defence Studies Centre (SDSC) at ANU for the next two decades.

She was a prolific author. She published eight major books, including *Negotiation from Strength: A Study in the Politics of Power* (1962), *The Debatable Alliance: An Essay in Anglo-American Relations* (1964), *The Conventions of Crisis: A Study in Diplomatic Management* (1971), *The Diplomacy of Détente: The Kissinger Era* (1977), *Dependent Ally: A Study in Australian Foreign Policy* (1984), and *A World Out of Balance: American Ascendancy and International Politics in the 21st Century* (2003). She edited five other books, published some twenty monographs, and wrote about seventy-five chapters in edited books and articles in academic journals. (A full list of her publications is included at the end of this volume). She was still working on five different papers at the time of her death.

This volume is divided into three parts. Part One describes Coral's personal constitution and provides an overview of her career. Chapter one, by her brother Harry Bell, recounts her early years. They were not easy. Her mother died when she was only seven years old, her father lost his job at the beginning of the Great Depression, and she was looked after by relatives during her primary school years. She was fifteen at the time of the Munich Crisis. She started at Sydney University just a few months before the Battle of the Coral Sea. She was worried that the presence of Japanese submarines in Sydney Harbour presaged a Japanese invasion, and worked with a degaussing unit at the National Physics Laboratory at Sydney University on techniques to protect Australian ships against magnetic mines. She later acknowledged that her life-long interest in international crises and her 'realist' perspective originated in this period. She had initially sought a career in the Australian Diplomatic Service, but as

Desmond Ball tells in chapter two, she ran afoul of a group in the Department of External Affairs who were spying for the Soviet Union and wanted her away from their predacity. Academia was essentially an accidental vocation.

Geoffrey Barker provides in chapter three a journalistic description of Coral. He describes her as 'perhaps Australia's most eminent and respected international security scholar' who 'was present at the creation of the post-War world of U.S.-Soviet superpower competition'. He recalls her 'scholarly modesty' and notes that 'she did not play the media game and seek to promote her views …. To her, international security issues were too profound to be reduced to the often glib formulas to which journalists seek to reduce complex issues'. She described her work as 'a sort of meditation on history'. Meredith Thatcher worked for Coral as a research assistant in the Strategic and Defence Studies Centre from 2002 to 2010, and describes her, in chapter four, from a quite different perspective. She notes that Coral was a very rare woman in a male-dominated profession, at least when Coral entered it. She characterises Coral as 'an optimistic realist', who was also compassionate, gracious, and humble, with 'a dry wit and warm personality'.

Robert O'Neill provides in chapter five a comprehensive overview of Coral's academic career. She obtained her doctorate at LSE in the early 1950s and then worked at Chatham House, where she enjoyed the tutelage of Martin Wight, and began her association with the founders of the International Institute for Strategic Studies (IISS) in London in the late 1950s, and then accepted a professorship at Sussex University in the 1970s. Her last three decades or so were spent with the Department of International Relations and the SDSC at ANU. O'Neill characterises her as a 'conservative realist', who shared the conservative political philosophy of Michael Oakeshott, but was opposed to the US (and Australian) intervention in Vietnam in the 1960s and early 1970s, critical of covert operations of the US Central Intelligence Agency (CIA) such as the overthrow of Iran's populist prime minister, Mohammad Mossadegh, in 1953, and despaired at the simplicity of the foreign policy views of successive conservative Australian governments. She was a fan of Henry Kissinger in the 1970s and applauded the way President Ronald Reagan dealt with the Soviet Union in the 1980s, but she later supported the basic approach to international affairs articulated by President Barack Obama, who she praised for recognising that the world had undergone a 'profound, irreversible redistribution of power' towards Asia.[1]

Most of Coral's academic career was spent in Departments of International Relations, but she was always more interested in critiques of policy rather than

1   Coral Bell, 'Seven Years to Get it Right', *American Review*, November 2009, http://americanreviewmag. com/stories/Seven-years-to-get-it-right (accessed 11 November 2013).

International Relations theory. Indeed, she disdained theoretical approaches to the field.[2] Nevertheless, as the contributions to Part Two of this volume show, she inevitably possessed a theoretical framework, albeit rarely explicated and somewhat inchoate. In chapter six, Ian Hall argues that 'her international thought', which he calls an 'agent-centred interpretive theory of international relations', was actually quite sophisticated. She accepted from Martin Wight that the disciplines of philosophy, literature and history could 'capture truths about human societies', and that politics was best explained in terms of ideas (the beliefs and perceptions of policy-makers) and institutions (including conventions and norms of behaviour as much as formal institutions), with events being determined essentially by 'agency, contingency and contestability'. JDB ('Bruce') Miller, in chapter seven, reiterates this perspective. He notes that Coral 'brought a practical and sophisticated analysis to the study of the international system', in which the beliefs of policy-makers, mediated through decision-making processes, are paramount. In chapter eight, James L Richardson locates her in 'classical realism, grounded in history and the humanities', not at all deterministic but providing great scope for political and diplomatic choice.

Part Three moves from international relations to the realm of power politics, which Coral explored with respect to practical policy-making concerning such critical matters as crisis management, Cold War competition, alliance diplomacy, US and Australian foreign and defence policies, and the construction of a stable and sustainable international system. In chapter nine, Brendan Taylor relates that she was a devoted Australian, always conscious, in her own words, of 'her own country's efforts to provide for its future security', and that this laid ultimately in the durability of 'the central balance' between the great powers, and Australia's alliance with a principal power in this 'balance'.[3] He is greatly impressed by her unremitting sense of optimism and her 'unrelenting drive to look imaginatively toward the future'. He notes that as far back as the 1960s, in *The Debatable Alliance*, she was already searching for alternative power-sharing arrangements, developing the concept of a 'shadow condominium'.[4]

In chapter ten, Michael Wesley examines Coral's interpretation of the Cold War. He notes that her 'first professional engagement with international affairs was as a practitioner' in government service and that this had 'a lasting impact on her work'. Moreover, this formative period coincided with the beginning of the Cold War, which she watched closely through to its end. He stresses her intuitive capacity, which allowed her, 'without being cased in ... ponderous methodology', but nevertheless grounded in fecund concepts, to portray the

2   Coral Bell, 'The State of the Discipline: I.R.', *Quadrant*, vol 12, no. 1, January-February 1968, p. 82.

3   Coral Bell, *The Asian Balance of Power: A Comparison with European Precedents*, Adelphi Paper no. 44, International Institute for Strategic Studies, London, February 1968, p. 1.

4   Coral Bell, *The Debatable Alliance: An Essay in Anglo-American Relations*, Chatham House Essays No. 3, Oxford University Press, London, 1964, pp. 108-113.

Cold War and its outcome primarily in terms of the characters, beliefs and judgements of the key policy-makers involved. Over the long term, the US emerged victorious because it proved better able to 'negotiate power'.

In chapter eleven, Robert Ayson reviews Coral's work on crisis management. He notes at the outset that she was concerned with 'the ideas that could be gleaned from the practice of international diplomacy'. This 'made her more of a commentator than a theorist', but she was 'an exceptionally adroit commentator'. Crisis management for Coral was a fundamental alternative to catastrophic war. Wars have become potentially much more destructive, but they still flourish. Crises can only be managed by the parties to 'the central balance of power'. Only the dominant powers can affect 'central crises', and only they can prevent local crises from turning into central ones. The quality of crisis diplomacy is determinate, which in practice means the policy choices of the decision-makers of the dominant powers. Shared conventions, or patterns of behaviour, are more important than formal institutions. Power, represented by armed force, is crucial, but it is mediated by 'signals' (which communicate threats or offers to the other party to the crisis); shared conventions ensure that the signals are correctly understood by the respective decision-makers.

William Tow, in chapter twelve, reviews Coral's work on 'alliance politics', which includes her assessments of both US leadership of the Western alliance system and, more particularly, the functioning of the US-Australia alliance. Again, diplomatic history rather than international relations theory was her main instrument in these endeavours. With regard to US leadership, she appreciated by the early 2000s, following the terrorist attack on the US homeland in September 2011 and the 'ineffectual US invasion and occupation of Iraq' in 2003, that global power was inevitably being redistributed by 'economic, demographic and technological changes', as well as 'Jihadist challenges', and that this required new forms of alignment, but she remained persuaded that the US would 'remain the paramount power of the society of states' for the foreseeable future. With regard to the US-Australia alliance, she believed that by hosting US facilities such as Pine Gap, Australia had become less dependent on the US. The alliance had become 'considerably less unequal', transmuted into 'interdependence of a relatively symmetrical sort'.[5] She remained convinced that Australia would remain 'inextricably and beneficially tied to US power as the best means for ensuring its own national security and for pursuing global stability'; but she also believed that Australia could play a positive role in adjudicating US reconciliation of its Cold War bilateral alliance system with the burgeoning construction of multilateral institutions in the Asia-Pacific region.

---

5   Coral Bell, *Dependent Ally: A Study in Australian Foreign Policy*, 3rd edn, Allen & Unwin, Sydney, 1993, p. 183.

Hugh White brings together and develops the key themes articulated in earlier chapters in his culminating essay on 'The Concert of Power: Avoiding Armageddon'. He recapitulates the impact of strategic developments in Coral's formative years on her subsequent career—the destructiveness of the Second World War, the development and use of the atomic bomb, the practitioner's perspective on the workings of the international system, and the importance of diplomacy. She was an optimistic realist, believing that the policy-makers in the dominant states could reach and sustain modes of communication and agreements which could minimise the risks of war and hence avoid atomic Armageddon. Following on from Martin Wight and other members of the English School of International Relations and also the influence of Henry Kissinger, she moved from implicit support for notions of a 'shadow condominium' to being a dedicated advocate of a 'concert of powers'. In a conflict-ridden world, with nuclear weapons aplenty, only a concert in which power is shared in the over-riding interest of preventing major wars can avoid Armageddon. White agrees with this analysis, but believes that Coral underestimated the difficulties involved in the construction of such a concert. He concludes with the admonition that, precisely because avoidance of catastrophic war should be our highest priority, we should all—academics and policy-makers alike—devote our energies to overcoming those difficulties, especially with respect to achieving an accommodation between the US and China (and Asia's other great powers).

Finally, then, after hearing from more than a dozen of her friends and colleagues, it should be possible to say who Coral Bell was, what she was like, what she did, and what was her legacy. She in fact had many close friends, which attests to her charm, compassion, generosity and engaging personality. And she had many colleagues willing to write about her, which signifies that the things she did were both important and interesting.

Coral's legacy is difficult to summarise; it is primarily indirect, through her ideas and arguments. O'Neill reckons that 'her analytical legacy is a view of the world where US power and influence have been eroded through poorly thought-out policies and lack of understanding of the United States' own weakness in the first decade of this century'. It is surely broader than that, encompassing the whole discourse on power politics and international relations, including crisis management and alliance diplomacy, as well as other periods when US power was ascendant rather than eroding. As Taylor notes, her impact was frequently second-order, through 'the people she worked with, taught and mentored', and in particular, 'her education of a significant number of emerging scholars', many of whom subsequently took up 'senior positions in academia, government and the military'. An important legacy concerns gender, where she opened the path for women into the international politics field. For over half a century, 'ever since her appointment as one of Australia's first female diplomats, ... [she served] as a mentor and role model for female scholars and practitioners' in this field. Internationally, she lifted Australia's 'diplomatic profile'.

Unusually for academics, she attracted the respect of policy-makers from around the globe. Denis Healey, a founder of the IISS and the Secretary of State for Defence from 1964 to 1970 and Chancellor of the Exchequer from 1974 to 1979, observed, with her in mind, that 'from the middle fifties Australia has contributed more to international understanding of defence problems than any country of similar size'.[6] Henry Kissinger, former National Security Advisor and Secretary of State under President Richard Nixon, invoked her ideas in his own writings.[7] Sir Keith Waller, Australia's first career ambassador to the United States (1964-70) and Secretary of the Department of Foreign Affairs in Canberra (1970-74) said that 'her work has brought a new lustre to the reputation of Australia in all countries where people follow the serious study of foreign affairs'.[8] Kim Beazley, former Minister for Defence and leader of the Australian Labor Party, said in 2008 that Coral 'stood out' as one of the two scholars (the other being Hedley Bull) who had 'captured the attentions of policy practitioners'.[9] Her funeral was attended by former heads of the Australian Department of Defence and the Department of Foreign Affairs and Trade, the Defence Intelligence Organisation (DIO) and the Office of National Assessments (ONA).

She was clearly a realist, for whom power, relational and broadly defined, was the central concept in the functioning of the international system. But her realism was unique; she could be characterised not only as a 'conservative realist' or a 'classical realist', but also, a much rarer breed, an 'optimistic realist'. Indeed, she could be called a 'constructivist realist'. It has been said (by Ayson) that she was a commentator, not a theorist, but she was never content to be merely descriptive. Her commentaries were invariably *prescriptive*, stipulating how the international system (or statecraft, for agency was more important than structure) *should* function. In fact, adept statecraft can create sound structures. It has also been pointed out (by Wesley) that Coral emphatically opposed value-laden foreign policies, but not because she lacked values; rather, values were difficult to negotiate, whereas contests over power could be bargained and managed. In fact, contests over values were usually resolved by power contests anyway.

6   Denis Healey, *The Time of My Life*, Michael Joseph, London, 1989, p. 192.
7   See, for example, Henry Kissinger, *Does America Need a Foreign Policy?*, 2nd edn, Touchstone, New York, 2002, p. 288.
8   Cited in Coral Bell, *Crises and Australian Diplomacy*, Arthur F Yencken Memorial Lecture 1972, Australian National University Press, 1973, p. 1.
9   Kim Beazley, 'Thinking Security: Influencing National Strategy from the Academy; An Australian Experience', Coral Bell Lecture 2008, Lowy Institute for International Policy, Sydney, 19 March 2008, p. 5.

For Coral, the ultimate value was the avoidance of catastrophic war (or Armageddon) and the 'preservation of human life and human society' in a conflict-ridden world.[10] As Hall argues, she held 'a vision of international relations that was both human and humane'. In the end, she was a committed humanitarian.

Acknowledgements

Three of the chapters (those by JDB Miller, James L Richardson and Brendan Taylor) are more or less revised versions of articles published in the *Australian Journal of International Affairs* (AJIA), Volume 59, No. 3, September 2005. We are grateful to Professor Andrew O'Neil (Editor-in-Chief), Dr Tracey Arklay (Managing Editor), and Michelle Whittaker (Permissions and Licensing Administrator at the Routledge Taylor & Francis Group) for permission to reprint these articles.

An earlier version of Geoffrey Barker's chapter was published in the *Australian Financial Review Magazine* on 29 July 2005. Desmond Ball's chapter is a slightly revised version of an article originally published in *The Australian* on 14 January 2012.

The photograph on the front cover, as well as Plates 8 and 9, were taken at a lecture given by Coral at the Lowy Institute for International Policy in Sydney on 19 March 2008. Plate 10 was contributed by Dr Katherine Morton, Department of International Relations, ANU. Darren Boyd and Olivia Cable helped with the digital processing of some of the images. Harry and Hellen Bell, Coral's brother and sister-in-law, provided several of the photographs and were supportive of this project from the outset.

We are indebted to Dr Pauline Kerr for her valuable comments on an earlier version of our manuscript.

---

10   Coral Bell, *The Diplomacy of Détente: The Kissinger Era*, St. Martin's Press, New York, 1977, pp. 32-33.

Part 1: Coral Bell: The Person and the Scholar

1. Coral's Early Life

Harry Bell

I was about two and a half years of age, when our mother returned from Christmas shopping complaining of a headache, lay on a bed and passed away due to a cerebral haemorrhage. Coral was about seven years of age at the time.

Coral was born at Gladesville in Sydney on 30 March 1923. After this date we moved to Queanbeyan where I was born, and then returned to Sydney, living at Bondi, opposite Bondi Beach.

Our father had been an electrical contractor, but his business collapsed in 1930 and he was out of work for almost eight years. We grew up in a society dominated by the Great Depression. Our father never really recovered from the double blow of losing his wife and having to bring up three young children alone, with no money.

On the death of our mother, Coral was sent to live with our aunt (our mother's sister) and uncle, who owned the local hotel in Eden on the South Coast, and were quite well off. Coral later said that, having been sent to Eden, she had not only lost her mother but had also lost her two brothers and her father.

Coral attended a Catholic school in Eden, run by the Sisters of St Joseph, and did well scholastically. Coral proved to be a diligent student in Eden and, when she completed sixth class, aged about eleven, gained entry to the selective school, Sydney Girls High, and returned to live with us in Sydney. I had no memory of Coral before she returned.

When she completed sixth class she was awarded a bursary of twenty-five pounds per year to complete her Intermediate. When she completed her Intermediate, she gained eight straight 'A's and a bursary of fifty pounds per year. She completed her Leaving Certificate at Sydney Girls High, where her name appears on the Honour Roll, in 1941.

She won a scholarship which paid all her fees to attend Sydney University from 1942 to 1944, where she completed a Bachelor of Arts Degree. She joined the Department of External Affairs as a diplomatic cadet in early 1945.

During her years in high school and at university, she was very serious and very studious. As a teenager, she had some friendships with girls from school, but she was not a 'party girl'. As far as I know, she never had a boyfriend. She did not play any sports, and had no hobbies. She liked going to the movies and listening to classical music, but mainly she just studied.

2. From External Affairs to Academia: Coral's Encounter with the KGB's Spy Ring in Australia[1]

Desmond Ball

Coral Bell was one of the world's foremost academic experts on international relations and power politics. However, her life in academia was unintended. She had envisaged a vocation in international politics, but in some aspect of public service. Her move to academia was essentially an accidental by-product of a friendship with colleagues who were spying for the Soviet Union.[2]

She began her career in the Australian Diplomatic Service, joining the Department of External Affairs as a Diplomatic Cadet in Canberra in 1945. Over the next three years, she got to know well several members of the Department who were members of the Soviet spy ring, especially Jim Hill (code-named 'Tourist') and Ric Throssell ('Ferro'). She subsequently became 'absolutely persuaded' that John Burton, the head of the Department, 'provided top-cover' for the spies. She believed that an attempt was made to recruit her in late 1947, and that her caustic response caused Burton to move quickly to sideline her in the Department.

Coral recorded her recollections of this controversial period in an unpublished memoir, which I discussed further with her on 15 November 2011 and 10 January 2012. She described the general security situation in External Affairs at the time, as well as her own personal experience, in great detail.[3]

In 1946–48, External Affairs was one of several Departments housed in West Block, on the western side of Parliament House. 'In those days we were a very small group: the whole of the diplomatic staff [about 30 people] could fit into one medium-sized seminar-room'. Security in the building was appalling. 'In those innocent days, no one, from the Minister down [in fact particularly the Minister], was in the least security-minded. There were no guards about, and practically no locks or barriers within the building.' Bell recorded that the staff 'used in most cases to bring sandwiches for lunch, and eat them sprawled on the lawn outside the office, not even bothering to lock our rooms as we left

1   This is a revised version of Desmond Ball, 'Soviet Spies had Protection in Very High Places', *The Australian*, 14 January 2012.
2   Desmond Ball and David Horner, *Breaking the Codes: Australia's KGB Network, 1944–1950*, Allen & Unwin, Sydney, 1998.
3   Coral Bell, 'A Preoccupation with Armageddon', unpublished memoir, Canberra, 2012.

temporarily, though foreign diplomats roamed unescorted about the building'. She says that Dr Evatt, the Minister, 'not only did not believe in security; he despised security'.

In 1946, Bell was assigned to the United Nations Division of the Department, of which Burton was then the head as well as being head of the entire Department. Here she formed a close relationship with Hill and Throssell, her senior colleagues in the Division. 'I said I used to bring sandwiches for lunch, and eat them on the West Block lawn. And much of the time I had very pleasant company in the shapes of three agreeable young men, Jim Hill, Ric Throssell, and Fred Rose. Fred was an anthropologist who worked nearby, a great charmer who always seemed to be at everyone's parties'. Rose, who worked successively in the Department of Territories and the Department of Post-War Reconstruction, also worked for Soviet intelligence (code-named 'Professor').

At one of the lunches with Throssell, Hill and Rose in late 1947, after they had finished eating, Throssell said to Bell that, 'Some of us think that the Soviet Union ought to see these documents'. Bell said that, 'I assumed he was joking, so I laughed merrily, and said something to the effect that it sounded like a splendid way to get oneself into jail'.

Bell believed that Throssell told Burton of her 'frivolous' response, and that Burton 'acted fast' to remove her from his central policy division. 'A [week or two] after that carefree mention of jail, I had found myself transferred out of Dr Burton's UN Division to the Southeast Asia Division, so I saw less of the others. And again only a few months after that, in 1948, I was "posted" to the Australian office in New Zealand, so I never saw any of them again'. She resigned from the Department at the end of her term in Wellington in 1951, and moved to London to begin her illustrious academic career.

The 'documents' that were specifically referred to at the lunch were officially called Foreign Office Prints. They were important British Foreign Office dispatches and telegrams which were routinely distributed around the Foreign Office itself and to the Cabinet, other relevant government agencies in London, and the External Affairs Departments of a few Commonwealth countries. They were classified 'Confidential' rather than 'Secret' or 'Top Secret'. Jim Hill had already been providing this material to Soviet intelligence on a regular basis (every week or two) since at least September 1945. It was relatively low-level political reporting, although it gave Moscow a detailed picture of British foreign policy regarding numerous other countries and international issues.

Bell recalled the incident on the West Block lawn eight years later, in late 1955, when she was at Chatham House in London and read the section on Fred Rose and June Barnett in the Report of the Royal Commission on Espionage (the

Petrov Royal Commission). In April 1950, Barnett, who had only recently joined the UN Division, was invited to dinner by Rose at his home in Froggatt Street in Turner, where Rose introduced her to Walter Seddon Clayton, the 'spy-master' of the KGB's espionage network in Australia. Bell found that the arguments used by Rose to suborn Barnett included a 'precise sentence said to me, by Ric,' at the lunch in 1947.

Barnett's story raised with Bell 'the possibility that I might have been initially seen as a "possible recruit to the cause" by Ric and Fred and Jim, [and others higher up?]'; and that she 'had disappointed that expectation with my light-hearted remark about jail'. She also realised 'that my subsequent days in the Department might have been influenced by those circumstances'.

Bell firmly believed that Burton provided 'top-cover' for the spies in his Department. 'Someone in Moscow must have had a sense of humour, for the code-name given to the Department of External Affairs was "Nook", and it definitely appears to have been one, in its standard definition of "a sheltered place". But who was doing the sheltering? To my mind, [it was] Burton, not Evatt'.

Indeed, Bell believed that Burton was more involved with Soviet intelligence than merely his 'top-cover' role. In particular, she considered the possibility that Burton was the principal contact of the head of the Soviet military intelligence (GRU) office in the Canberra Embassy, Victor Zaitsev. She said, 'I wouldn't be in the least surprised'.

Bell recalled Rose with some fondness. She said he was 'such a nice person', and 'very charming'. She went to parties at his house in Turner, which were also attended by Throssell and Hill. In 1948 to 1950, this house was the main 'drop' used by the spies in External Affairs to leave documents and other material for collection by Clayton. For the previous three years, Clayton had used a flat in Braddon, occupied by Throssell from 1947 to 1949, for this purpose.

Bell believed that: 'The truly tragic figure in all this was to my mind Ric Throssell. When I first knew him, round 1947, he was a handsome young man with apparently everything to live for, and prospects of rising to whatever eminence he wanted, either in diplomacy or politics, or even literature. He used to read to us, during those lunchtimes, bits of a play he was writing, all about atomic weapons and such'.

Coral was a woman of high personal principles. Although she had often intimated to me over the previous two decades that she had more information to tell about Burton, Throssell and Hill than Horner and I had recounted in *Breaking the Codes,* she had wanted to withhold it until her memoirs were completed. She would not betray friends; she never lost affection for Rose and Throssell. She was always adamant, however, that the truth as she recollected it should eventually be told.

3. Coral Bell: A Preoccupation with Armageddon

Geoffrey Barker

In mid-2005 Coral Bell, aged eighty-two, sat with me in an Australian National University (ANU) conference room for more than two hours discussing her life and work as perhaps Australia's most eminent and respected international security scholar. A lengthy article based on our conversation was published on 29 July 2005 in *The Australian Financial Review Magazine*.[1] Coral later told me, 'You have made me famous'. In fact I had barely done justice to her, but I did not appreciate the extent of my inadequacy until early 2013 when I read her own short memoir entitled, 'A Preoccupation with Armageddon'—a marvellously insightful, witty, and personal account of her life and career.

It was not just that her writing was superior to my hasty journalism. It was also that I missed some key aspects of her life—most notably the approach to her, by colleagues in the old Department of External Affairs in 1947, that she act as a spy for the Soviet Union. The approach, which she laughed away, was subsequently revealed in January 2012 by Professor Desmond Ball in an article published in *The Australian* newspaper. I confess that I was overawed by the grey-haired grandmotherly figure with the white shawl over her shoulders sipping coffee with me: I had known and admired her work for many years and I had enjoyed her company when I was a Visiting Fellow at the ANU Strategic and Defence Studies Centre. I just didn't ask the right question at the time.

Now, following Coral's death in September 2012, I have the opportunity to revise and update *The Australian Financial Review Magazine* article for this publication. I hope I can serve her better in death than I could in life because Coral Bell deserves to be recognised and memorialised as a great international scholar who was present at the creation of the post-War world of US–Soviet superpower competition and who, to her last days, remained an astute analyst of the emerging post-Cold War world of rising state powers like China and India and non-state players like Jihadist terrorists. Coral Bell was a woman who understood and appreciated the complexities and contradictions of international relations. She understood the importance of history and of patience in dealing with international disputes and crises. Her views were conservative and realist, but of the English realist school labelled 'rationalism' which sought to blend

---

1   This is a revised version of Geoffrey Barker, 'The Analyst', *The Australian Financial Review Magazine*, 29 July 2005.

the pessimism of realism with the optimism of liberal internationalism. She remained fundamentally optimistic about the future of the world because, as she said, 'I have seen far more dangerous times'.

Unlike many of her colleagues Coral did not pursue public recognition. She did not play the media game and seek to promote her views. That scholarly modesty might explain why it was not until 2005 that Coral received her Order of Australia in the Queen's Birthday Honours. To her, international security issues were too profound to be reduced to the often glib formulas to which journalists seek to reduce complex issues. 'My work is a sort of meditation on history', she told me. 'History is what you have to be guided by. You can't change everything overnight and history teaches the necessity for patience'. She also recalled with approval the words of the great conservative philosopher Michael Oakeshott that international politics was about maintaining an even keel in 'a boundless and bottomless sea' where there were no safe harbours.[2]

Bell's optimism was reinforced by the fact that she had, as she said, 'grown up when the world was preparing for war'. 'I think on the whole there has been a very great improvement in the way people think. The world was far more dangerous during the outbreak of war in 1939 and at the beginning of the Cold War in 1946 that it is at present. That's because we survived the Second World War. In the years between 1946 and 1989 we survived the very great dangers of the bipolar nuclear world with the tension between the United States and the Soviet Union. In 1962 and 1983 the world was very close to the brink. I don't see any such closeness at the moment'.

'The Jihadists are an awful problem, of course, but they are not as devastating a problem as nuclear war between the great powers', Bell said. 'We calculated there would be 300 million dead in the first 60 minutes if there were all-out war between the US and Soviet Union. That's a reason for an optimistic view. We have survived all that and I think we can survive a lot more'.

To the end of her life Bell's realism attracted her to the notion that a European-style concert of powers could preserve peace more effectively than the so-called balance of powers that underpins standard realism. Her two late papers *Living with Giants* and *The End of the Vasco da Gama Era* both argued for a concert of powers to oversee the re-emerging multi-polar world of large and powerful states, especially in the Asia-Pacific region.[3] It is a fascinating and controversial view that is still being debated in realist circles.

---

2 See Michael Oakeshott, 'Political Education', Inaugural Lecture delivered at the London School of Economics and Political Science, 6 March 1951.

3 See Coral Bell, *Living with Giants: Finding Australia's Place in a More Complex World,* Strategy Report, Australian Strategic Policy Institute, Canberra, April, 2005; and *The End of the Vasco da Gama era: The Next Landscape of World Politics,* Lowy Institute Paper 21, Lowy Institute for International Policy, Sydney, 2007.

Coral Mary Bell was born in Sydney in 1923, the middle child and only daughter of a poor Anglo-Irish family. Her mother died when she was seven and her father, an electrical contractor who was out of work for almost eight years during the depression, sent her to live with relatives at Eden on the south coast of NSW where she attended St Joseph's convent school and later returned to attend Sydney Girls High School.

The nuns at Eden taught Bell what she called 'the most useful lesson I ever had'. The nuns taught what Bell remembered as 'a very Catholic version of history', but she knew that state examiners would expect a Protestant version. 'So at age eleven', she said, 'I still remember cheerfully describing a fourteenth century character called Wycliffe as 'the morning star of the reformation' for my Protestant examiners and as a 'dissolute and heretic monk' for my Catholic examiners. Complexity did not intimidate Coral Bell.

From a young age Bell started bumping into the historical crises that ensured her work was informed by much more than reports and texts. She recalled the 1938 Munich Crisis as 'the first event in the history of my times to affect me intellectually and emotionally'. 'My preoccupation with crisis as diplomatic process began there … and I've been writing about it ever since', she said. Bell heard the explosions and gunfire when Japanese mini-submarines attacked Sydney in June 1942 and she had a vivid memory of hearing of the atomic bomb attack on Japan in August 1945, the year in which she graduated in Arts from Sydney University. As she said in her private memoir: 'I have never been, in any of its senses, a party girl …'.

During the war, while a university student, this serious young woman had a job doing secret work for the navy in the university's national physics laboratory degaussing (demagnetising) warships to protect them from mines. Just down the corridor from where she worked other scientists and engineers were working on radio location (radar) devices. She saw this experience as a key to her career. 'For three war years I spent my days surrounded by scientists and technicians. I think the reason I took to strategic studies was that I had started in the field of weaponry. Degaussing and radio location were things for the troops. I think I acquired a certain interest in strategic hardware at the time. Likewise, an empiricist mindset which is still with me', she said.

Having read mainly English, history and philosophy, in 1944 Bell sat an examination for admission to the new diplomatic service being set up by the External Affairs Minister Dr Herbert Vere ('Doc') Evatt. She was the only woman in an intake of ten cadets which included Donald Horne (briefly) and the legendary public servants Bill Pritchett and Bob Furlonger. It was an age of innocence at the Department of External Affairs. Bell recalled that there was no security. 'We left our offices open when we went to lunch which we would eat on the lawns outside while foreign diplomats were allowed to wander unescorted around the building. Things were very primitive', she said.

Bell spent six years at External Affairs working mainly on policy surrounding the founding of the United Nations and ANZUS (Australia New Zealand United States) Treaty. In 1948 she was posted to New Zealand which she said felt like being awarded 'the wooden spoon' although the posting was 'reasonably interesting'. It was while Bell was working in the United Nations Division of External Affairs in Canberra that she received the espionage approach from colleagues she described in her memoir as 'rather charming spies' who she 'assumed to be friends'.

They were Fred Rose, an anthropologist and open Communist Party member, and External Affairs colleagues Jim Hill, brother of communist leader Ted Hill, and Ric Throssell, son of well-known communist Katharine Susannah Prichard. One day, after lunch, Throssell said to Bell, 'some of us think that the Soviet Union ought to see these documents'. Bell wrote, 'I assumed he was joking so I laughed merrily and said something to the effect that it sounded like splendid way to get oneself into jail'. Professor Desmond Ball, who reported this exchange after conversations with Bell, wrote that Bell believed Throssell told Burton of her 'frivolous' response and that Burton 'acted fast' to remove her from his central policy division. 'Bell firmly believes that Burton provided "top cover" for the spies in his department', Ball wrote. In her memoir Bell describes Burton as 'the most controversial and ambiguous' of the three intellectually dominant young officials in External Affairs (the others were Paul Hasluck and Arthur Tange). She also writes that she believes Burton, not Evatt, was 'doing the sheltering' of the Communist spies in the Department. But despite her apparent suspicions, she stops short of making the contentious and contested claim that Burton was himself a spy.

In 1951, Bell resigned from the External Affairs department feeling, she said, 'like a cog in a large machine' and sailed to the UK to study at the London School of Economics (LSE) and to embark on her extraordinary career as a university teacher and researcher. She did not marry. 'In my day you were told that if you married you were deemed to have resigned from the diplomatic service. So I gave up the idea', she said. Like so many of her contemporaries, war claimed her first sweetheart. In a brief moment of undisguised sadness Bell told me:, 'He was killed during a landing in Papua New Guinea. They told me he was shot in the head and died instantly without suffering. I hope that is true'.

At LSE she was an evening student doing research work during the day at the Royal Institute of International Affairs. Working with the historian Arnold J

Toynbee she wrote the Institute's *Survey of International Affairs for 1954*.[4] Bell admired Toynbee, describing him to me as 'splendid, delightful, loyal, modest, diffident'. It was at the LSE too that she came under the influence of the noted English international relations theorist Martin Wight whom she called 'the chief intellectual influence of my life'. She was present when the conservative Michael Oakeshott took over the LSE leadership following the retirement of the socialist Harold Laski. Among her colleagues was Karl Popper whose great book *The Open Society and Its Enemies* she greatly admired.

Appointed the first international relations lecturer at Manchester University in 1956 Bell started work on her PhD on the US Cold War strategy labelled *Negotiation from Strength*.[5] A Rockefeller Fellowship took her to the US where she met the giants who created the modern bipolar world—George Kennan, the author of the US containment policy, Dean Acheson and Paul Nitze. And J Robert Oppenheimer, the father of the atomic bomb who, she said, gave her the first clue about US strategy in the nuclear world when he directed her to a top secret document written by Nitze. Bell said Oppenheimer 'looked like a being from outer space'. He had lost his security clearances due to past communist associations and was less discreet than some others, she said. Bell's work was later much admired by Henry Kissinger.

In 1961 Bell was appointed the first Senior Lecturer in International Relations at the University of Sydney. She returned to England to a Readership at the LSE in 1965 and in 1972 was appointed Professor of International Relations at the University of Sussex. In 1977 she returned to The Australian National University 'to spend my last ten years before retirement in my native land and in a research appointment'. From 1988 until her death she was a Visiting Fellow at the ANU Strategic and Defence Studies Centre where, to her last days, she continued to hone her craft as a compelling lecturer and a prolific and elegant writer. 'I suppose', she wrote in her memoir, 'I was one of the last generation to feel one could pursue a career on both sides of the world without any conflict of loyalties'.[6]

In his 2003 Boyer Lecture, Professor Owen Harries spoke about Coral's 'ability to cope with and enjoy complexity', he said: 'there is nothing simplistic or crude about her analysis'. To ANU Professor Emeritus Paul Dibb, Bell is simply, 'one of the great unrecognised and unsung strategic experts in this country. During the Cold War, she did absolutely magnificent work on the central balance between the US and Soviet Union and what she called the 'signalling' in their relations.'

---

4   *Survey of International Affairs for 1954*, Oxford University Press, London, 1956.
5   See Coral Bell, *Negotiation from Strength: A Study in the Politics of Power*, Chatto & Windus, London, 1962, and Alfred A. Knopf, New York, 1963.
6   Coral Bell, 'A Preoccupation with Armageddon, unpublished memoir, Canberra, 2012.

In a handsome tribute to Bell, Henry Kissinger wrote in his book, *Does America Need a Foreign Policy*: 'The Australian scholar Coral Bell has brilliantly described America's challenge: to recognise its own pre-eminence but to conduct its policy as if it were still living in a world of many centres of power'.[7] Australia and the world are poorer for the loss of her wisdom, judgement and insight.

---

7   Henry Kissinger, *Does America Need a Foreign Policy: Toward a Diplomacy for the 21st Century,* Simon & Schuster, New York, 2001.

4. Coral Bell: Recollections of an Optimistic Realist

Meredith Thatcher

Eighty-nine years separate Coral Bell's birth on 30 March 1923 from her death on 26 September 2012, but how Coral spent those years was, quite simply, remarkable. In one lifetime, she lived more than two. Despite earlier hardships and coming of age at the end of the Second World War, Coral's optimism about the outcome of world-shaping events never waned. With a pragmatic lens, she looked through her glasses clearly, never dimmed. She was, I believe, an optimistic realist.

Coral lived her life in three parts: her youth (spent mostly in New South Wales), her academic career (spent overseas and in Australia), and her twilight years (in semi-retirement, spent mostly at home and at The Australian National University).

When asked to contribute to this volume, I selected some of Coral's writings that were sitting on my shelf and considered my options: an academic essay or a personal recollection. Other contributors to this volume write of Coral's early years and her stellar academic career and impact on the international and domestic stage. I have chosen to offer a snapshot of Coral's recollections of her school and university years and time abroad, and of my own time knowing Coral during her later years in Canberra. The chapter ends with the eulogy I gave at her funeral.

Forging Connections

Sometimes you connect with a person instantly, and so it was when I first met Coral in August 2002. Coral may have been in her late seventies by then, but it was her computer that brought us together for the first time. I had just started working at the ANU Strategic and Defence Studies Centre (SDSC), while Coral was spending part of her working day at the Centre and part at home in Downer. At the time she was untangling the complexities of and linkages in the multipolar world that would be the focus of *A World Out of Balance*,[1] and

---

1   Coral Bell, *A World Out of Balance: American Ascendancy and International Politics in the 21st Century*, Longueville Books, Sydney, 2003. The Lowy Institute for International Policy launched the book on 4 March 2004 at the State Library of New South Wales.

talking of a concert of powers. Yet figuring out how to use her computer was proving harder to crack. Some would have opted out, staying with pen and paper. Not Coral. She never got frustrated, choosing instead to see the rapid changes in technology as just another hurdle to overcome. So we joined forces with her: the Centre's then-administrator Anne Dowling, the rest of the SDSC team, and the IT team in the College all coming to her aid.

Coral was highly intelligent, as the writings about her in this volume attest, but it was her dry wit and warm personality that were infectious. You can admire a person with a razor-sharp mind: the exceptional person is one with such a mind who is also diplomatic, humble and empathetic. Coral never sought awards, fame or fortune. She spent her life in service: furthering our thinking on weighty topics, inspiring students, and communicating with colleagues. Most of all, even when living abroad, she spent her life in service of Australia.

Turning Points

For Coral 'the Past is a foreign country' was relevant to Australia. She had grown up in a society still dominated by the Great Depression. She was fifteen when she started writing essays on international crises. A wonderful teacher at Sydney Girls High School encouraged her to view current events as history waiting to be written, so Coral wrote an essay on the Munich Crisis of 1938. But it was in two exams to enter high school that Coral was faced with writing a paper on the same topic. She chose to do so from differing perspectives. Coral regarded this moment as 'the most valuable lesson of her life'. In the understanding of wars and crises 'one must have some understanding of "where each side is coming from", and how the history of the whole conflict looks to them'. Turning points in history was a theme that Coral would return to again and again throughout her life.[2]

After high school, during the Second World War, Coral studied at the University of Sydney and spent time at a physics laboratory sited on campus. She was one of three people in a team that degaussed ships (neutralised their magnetic field) to protect them from magnetic mines. Others at the CSIRO Division of Radiophysics were working on developing radar. In the days before computing, 'practically back in the Ice Age' as she put it, her calculations were done on graph paper and with slide rule. So it was that, between 1942 and 1945, Coral spent almost all her waking hours doing war work, surrounded by physicists. In the evenings she attended lectures on history, literature, economics and

---

2   One of Dr Bell's research themes was turning points in history and she started her Introduction to her Lowy Institute power, *The End of the Vasco da Gama Era*, with the words, 'The next landscape of world politics is just beginning to be visible through the lingering twilight of the unipolar world'.

philosophy. The war made living austere, but Coral took to university life from the start. She had found an intellectual home and considered seminar rooms and libraries to be 'my natural habitat'.

Towards the end of the war, Coral contemplated her career options. She passed the exams to enter the diplomatic service and in early 1945 travelled to Canberra. At the time the capital offered minimal accommodation (with hostels for most new arrivals) and few social opportunities. As Coral said, 'visiting nearby Queanbeyan was rated a big day out'. Coral walked and caught buses, and it was not until she was posted to Wellington, New Zealand, that she got a driver's licence.

We always remember where we are when life-changing or momentous events happen. Coral said the reason for her work revolving around wars and crises (what Coral called 'my preoccupation with the possibility of Armageddon and how to avoid it') dated back to the day a fellow diplomatic cadet rushed in to tell her that an atomic bomb had destroyed Hiroshima. What always kept this event to mind was remembering the pattern of the hearth-rug she was standing on when she heard the news.

Yet of all the changes in Australia and the world that Coral chronicled she saw the 'status of (and rules for)' women in the workplace 'as the most radical'. She entered the Australian diplomatic service in an age when there were few female diplomats, and she recalled being told that she would have to resign if she chose to marry. Even after leaving the service, she selected a field of study then not often undertaken by women. In many respects Coral was a pioneer—ahead of her time by twenty to thirty years.

Today the diplomatic corps is larger than when she was a member—a time when all the staff could fit into a medium-sized seminar room. The small group meant that, even as a junior diplomat, Coral's work was varied and complex. In 1948 she was 'posted' to the Australian office in Wellington. She found the posting 'reasonably interesting' and the people she met 'able and amiable'. She attended balls at Government House, dinner at the Soviet Embassy, and many luncheons. In one notable episode, she found herself at a diplomatic function at the US Embassy. Having just learned to play golf, but never having played croquet, she swung her mallet back over her shoulder 'in my best golf style. The ball sailed over a group of trees and landed in the lake. There was a pained silence'.

The social side of diplomatic life was not, to quote Coral, 'my cup of tea'. She said she had never been 'a party girl, and diplomacy is a very party-ridden occupation, especially in a small post, as Wellington then was'. She noted, 'If you meet roughly the same fifty or so people at cocktail and dinner parties five evenings a week, you tend to run out of small-talk, which has never been my favourite form of conversation anyway'. Anyone who knew Coral can confirm that idle chitchat was not her way to communicate.

Coral needed a 'more reflective kind of life', and in 1951 she applied for study leave without pay. When this was refused, she resigned from diplomatic service. A life of travel, research, teaching and writing was to follow.

Beyond the Horizon

Coral's mind never stood still and neither did she. In the decade I knew her she moved house four times in Canberra: first from a house in Downer to a unit in O'Connor, then to retirement villages in Deakin and Ainslie. How she moved was by car and tales of Coral's style of parking and her driving to and from the Centre became legend. If she nudged a pole too much, she would state matter-of-factly, 'only a slight bingle'.

These days we take the speed of travel for granted. In the age of jets, we often forget the main modes of travel of the past, by ship across oceans and by train across continents. When Coral left for London in 1951, 'taking the slow boat' meant the journey was a destination in itself. She spoke of the fun aboard ship, and visiting exotic, unfamiliar port towns and cities. One photograph from that trip has her astride a camel, visiting the pyramids in Egypt.

The war was half a decade past when Coral arrived in London. She thought the city had 'a melancholy romantic charm. The cathedral then still stood among a wilderness of ruins, which were overgrown by a pretty pink-blossomed wildflower called rose-bay willow herb, or London Pride. It all looked wonderfully symbolic'.

A few weeks after her arrival Coral moved into a shared flat in Kensington, and got her ration-book and first week's rations 'for three shillings and ten pence'. The rations were 'one chop, two eggs, a square of cheese barely enough to bait a mouse-trap, and a cube of butter about the size of a postage stamp, along with an ounce or so of tea and sugar'. She immediately missed the food from home. Coral's friend in the Royal Australian Air Force persuaded a friend who was flying aircraft back to England to bring her a case of tiny cans of condensed cream. With some brisk bartering, 'a lot more dinner tables than mine rejoiced in apple pie with real cream'. Coral supplemented the meagre rations with meals at the London School of Economics (LSE), which was to become the centre of her life for her first years in England.

She absorbed the political upheavals of the time, viewing the appointment of Michael J Oakeshott at LSE as 'a straw in the winds of change in the general intellectual climate of the world'.[3] While at LSE, she met Martin Wight. He was to become Coral's friend and colleague and 'the chief intellectual influence of my entire life'. Geoffrey Goodwin, another of Coral's lecturers, introduced her to Chatham House (or the Royal Institute of International Affairs)—'a second major influence on the way I saw the world'. At Chatham House she became rapporteur of the research study groups.[4] A group's meeting usually began in late afternoon and lasted through dinner until people had to leave to catch their train or drive or walk home. At Chatham House she met 'the rising stars of both sides of politics', who 'were willing to come and talk frankly'. The small (about twelve people) informal meetings gave Coral the opportunity to meet people she would not otherwise have met, including the founders of the International Institute for Strategic Studies (years before its founding in 1958). At Chatham House Coral met Arnold J Toynbee, a man she described as 'a most delightful old gentleman, everyone's favourite scholarly grandfather'. Toynbee was the editor of the annual *Survey of International Affairs* when Coral wrote the 1954 issue.[5] When Geoffrey Barraclough took over Toynbee's role in 1956, Coral applied for a Lectureship in Government at the University of Manchester.

Once appointed to the position, she moved to northwest England. At the university she came to appreciate one of what she later called 'the antique pleasures of university life … the conversation of the Senior Common Room'. Those gathered in that room would 'bounce ideas from their respective fields of expertise off each other'. It was at the University of Manchester that Coral began to develop her research into managing international crises by avoiding war and into managing defeat without recourse to war. Coral's professor was WJM ('Bill') Mackenzie, who had been appointed Chair of Government and Administration in 1948. He 'built up an outstanding Government Department which until the early 1960s was the best in Britain and gained an international reputation. He did it by spotting talent: from Aberdeen to Oxford'.[6] He 'created a culture, not of publish or perish, but of intellectual excitement and keeping abreast of developments in the discipline in the United States. In the early 1950s his young colleagues were pioneers in studies of voting behaviour, community power, pressure groups and developing countries. He had a remarkable instinct

---

3   Michael J Oakeshott (11 December 1901–19 December 1990) became Professor of Political Science at LSE in 1948, succeeding Harold J Laski (30 June 1893–24 March 1950). Oakeshott retired from LSE in 1969.

4   A person appointed by an organisation to report on the proceedings of its meetings.

5   Arnold J Toynbee (14 April 1889–22 October 1975) was Director of Studies at the Royal Institute of International Affairs (RIIA) in Chatham House between 1929 and 1956. He edited the annual *Survey of International Affairs* from 1920 to 1946.

6   See Dennis Kavanagh, 'Obituary: Professor W. J. M. Mackenzie', *The Independent*, 27 August 1996. www. independent.co.uk/news/people/obituary-professor-wjm-mackenzie-1311688.html (accessed 16 September 2013).

for where the subject was heading'.[7] As the originators of containment were mostly based in Washington, Coral asked Mackenzie to back her application for a Rockefeller Fellowship.[8] Once awarded, in early 1958 Coral left for the United States.

Upon her arrival, Coral found that the convivial atmosphere and 'intellectual excitement' in discussions over coffee hardly existed. Academics were so pressured to write that they 'drank their coffee in their rooms, with one hand on the typewriter'. Coral believed an academic's life should be half spent teaching and half spent doing research. She felt privileged to have known 'the system in its golden day' when academics faced few pressures. While in Washington, in late May 1959 Coral saw the funeral procession of former US Secretary of State John Foster Dulles. A few days later she began her travels around the country— to the Institute for Advanced Study, Princeton University, Princeton, NJ, to interview Robert Oppenheimer and to Harvard University, Cambridge, MA, to interview Henry Kissinger, a young professor there at the time.[9] Coral then set out for new territory by train: travelling across the north to San Francisco, then back across the south to New York. The trains were quite luxurious, and she enjoyed watching the scenery through the sight-seeing domes. While at Yellowstone National Park in 1959 she was caught in a 'minor' earthquake and had to travel on by bus.[10] The convoy stopped at every small bridge in the park to allow the passengers to walk across before re-boarding the buses. After the three months of travel Coral ended up at Columbia University in New York for the September re-opening of the academic year.

Coming Home

Once her research was complete, Coral sailed back to England. When she returned to the University of Manchester at the start of term, she learned that her father had died of a heart attack in Australia (about the time she was embarking for the voyage back to England) and she had missed his funeral.

Coral turned her research into the book *Negotiation from Strength: A Study in the Politics of Power*.[11] She continued to teach as a Lecturer in Government,

---

7   Kavanagh, 'Obituary: Professor W. J. M. Mackenzie'.
8   Coral Bell spent her time on the Rockefeller Fellowship at the School of Advanced International Studies at John Hopkins University in Washington, DC, and Columbia University in New York.
9   Between 1954 and 1959 Henry Alfred Kissinger was a member of the Harvard faculty in the Department of Government and the Center for International Affairs.
10   Yellowstone National Park recorded a series of earthquakes from 17 August 1959. The first earthquake (also known as the Hebgen Lake earthquake) measured 7.3–7.5 on the Richter magnitude scale. With her gift for understatement, Coral called this 'minor'.
11   Coral Bell, *Negotiation from Strength: A Study in the Politics of Power*, Chatto & Windus, London, 1962, and Alfred A. Knopf, New York, 1963.

remaining at the university until 1961.[12] But the call of Australia was strong, so she decided to leave for home. Her first appointment was as Senior Lecturer in Government at her *alma mater*, the University of Sydney, and she lived in a small flat at Double Bay, 'a long time before it became fashionable'. Coral's travels had taken her around the world to acclaim, and she would continue to garner accolades as her career continued at institutions such as the University of Sydney (1961–65), London School of Economics (1965–72), University of Sussex (1972–77), and The Australian National University (1977 until her death).

At 10:30am on 2 September 2005 I watched Coral Bell receive her much-deserved Order of Australia (Officer in the General Division) at Government House in Canberra. I was honoured to be one of the three people Coral chose to accompany her to this prestigious occasion; the others being a close Australian friend Betty MacFarlane, and another New Zealander Brendan Taylor, now the Head of the Strategic and Defence Studies Centre at ANU. The citation in the Investiture booklet reads: 'Dr Coral Bell: For service to scholarship and to teaching as a leading commentator and contributor to foreign and defence policy debate internationally and in Australia'.[13] Few people at the gathering knew Coral's work, yet there was an audible murmur when the then-Governor-General Philip Michael Jeffrey mentioned Henry Kissinger when speaking about Coral.

Reflecting on an Intellectual Giant

In 2005 just after Coral's book *A World out of Balance* was published,[14] Verona Burgess wrote an article in *The Canberra Times*. She started with the paragraph, 'Coral Bell might look as if she belongs in the knitting circle, but she has just published her newest book on global politics—sixty years after she first joined the Australian Diplomatic Corps in the era of the legendary 'Doc' Evatt'.[15]

When you conversed with Coral, you knew you were in the presence of an intellectual giant. Her ability to place events and patterns of thinking in context was admired greatly. She was able to stand back from any topic to get full view. She and I chatted in depth about education, history, politics, international crises, research, and writing. I even had the privilege to co-edit with Coral a book entitled *Remembering Hedley*, a compilation of recollections about Professor Hedley Bull and his work.[16]

---

12 Coral's academic qualifications were BA (Sydney, 1945), MSc Econ (London, 1954), and PhD (London, 1962).
13 Investiture booklet for 2 September 2005, Government House, Canberra, p. 5.
14 Coral Bell, *A World Out of Balance*.
15 Verona Burgess, 'US-style World Power "Not Seen Since the Days of the Romans"', *Canberra Times*, 5 February 2004, p. 4.
16 Coral Bell and Meredith Thatcher (eds), *Remembering Hedley*, ANU E Press, Canberra, 2008.

When I visited Coral in her residence in the Canberra suburb of O'Connor, we sometimes bought fish and chips for dinner. With much of her life spent overseas, Coral's favourite fish was barramundi. It brought back memories of her youth. When she moved into Goodwin Village in Ainslie, she couldn't wait until the social areas were built and we could lunch there. Until then we chatted over a roast meal at the nearby Ainslie Football & Social Club.

Coral kept minimal possessions, but she had a chair ready for whoever might drop in. Among her prized possessions were books and journals, including a bookcase full of *The National Interest* to which she contributed. She listened to radio and watched television less than she wrote, but always kept up with the news (usually ABC and SBS). She tried never to miss one of her favourite programs—the PBS NewsHour. If I was visiting, we would watch it together and debate the topics. Sometimes we agreed; sometimes we would agree to disagree. That's how it is with friends. Yet Coral had an even temperament and never raised her voice. Being so reasoned, she could make any disagreement a pleasurable experience. She never got cross, yet the one pastime we could never reconcile was crosswords and similar puzzles. I am a fan of them; Coral was not. She wisely spent her time on less frivolous endeavours.

Doing even the smallest task for Coral was a privilege. Towards the end of her life, Coral's mind stayed strong but her body became frail. She relented to using a walking stick and taking an arm when necessary as my brother Greg and I helped her with the weekly grocery shop. To my great regret, distance separated us in her final two years. But I visited her once and we corresponded by 'snail mail', her words always elegantly penned in flowing, open, cursive script.

Coral felt that today few opportunities exist for staff and students to sit down to discuss international and strategic affairs: the pressures of academic administration on the one hand and the need to pay off students loans on the other are simply too great. Her greatest wish towards the end of her life was that professors and others with long careers at a university might have a residence (even just one room) on campus where they could live the rest of their days. Coral had seen this while in England—the benefit of having easy access to chat with former colleagues and to continue enjoying university life after retirement. Lacking this environment she established a group at Goodwin, at first with few participants and Coral chairing the sessions. As word spread through the village that this new group discussed international affairs and the like, attendance increased rapidly and Coral started to share her chairing duties. I believe that underpinning Coral's intellectual pursuits was the need to always stay connected. I quote the words of Minh Bui Jones—a sentiment that echoes what I saw in her. Upon hearing of Coral's passing, he wrote:

It's a rare thing in an international relations expert to possess a balance of theory and experience, history and imagination, realism and hope. … She brought an antipodean temperament and perspective to the great questions of our time; she was our George Kennan in thick glasses, blue floral dress, white sneakers and a string of pearls.[17]

I conclude this chapter with my eulogy, without amendment, as delivered at Coral's funeral in Canberra in late 2012.

Last Words for a Wise and Gentle Soul

As we gather in Canberra today, it seems fitting to start with an acronym: CORAL—Compassionate, Original, Remarkable, Astute, and Loyal. To these qualities, I would add gracious, humble and independent.

Coral mapped out and chartered her own life, sacrificing much as she sailed across oceans to unfamiliar horizons and back. Yet she always steered a centre course on an even keel—a lesson learned when very young. Coral said that she learned her most valuable lesson in history at age eleven. This was when a decision needed to be made about whether she would attend a Catholic high school, some distance away from home, or a public school in Sydney. The only way to decide was for Coral to sit the Catholic Diocesan exams and the State school exams. As you would expect, she sailed through both—until she reached the history essay. As Coral put it, 'the convent she was attending taught a narrative rather heavily oriented to the woes of Ireland; the state schools rather heavily oriented to the glories of the British imperial story'.[18] What to do? For Coral, even at age eleven, it meant charting a course of what she called 'double think'—describing fourteenth century John Wycliffe as the 'morning star of the Reformation' for her Protestant examiners, and a 'dissolute and heretic monk' for her Catholic examiners. Coral said that 'such was her precocious ease with this post-modernist approach that, for her Catholic history, she won the Diocesan gold medal—and for her Protestant history, a place at Sydney Girls High School'.

In this tale we see a first glimpse of not only Coral's ability to stand tall and navigate through dilemmas, but her tolerance and ability to see events from differing perspectives. Not only was Coral elegant; the way she could weave the threads of disparate thoughts and patterns together into a cohesive fabric was also elegant. Discussions with Coral were never dull. You always felt the

---

17   Minh Bui Jones, 'On Coral's Calmness', *The Interpreter*, Lowy Institute, 5 October 2012: www.lowyinterpreter.org/post/2012/10/05/On-Corals-calmness.aspx (accessed 16 September 2013).
18   Coral Bell, as noted in her unpublished memoir, 'A Preoccupation with Armageddon'.

penetrating feelers of intellect entering your mind. Always weighing the options and giving measured yet thought-provoking responses, Coral continued to discover more and to question more—to the end.

Coral wrote to me saying that she was content with her decision to move to Goodwin. She liked the village atmosphere—the exchange of greetings when out for walks. She enjoyed greatly the group that discussed international relations. Most of all, Coral remained optimistic about the future for players on the international stage. She said she liked the 'delicate, ironic scepticism and pragmatism' of Michael Joseph Oakeshott. Indeed terms that might have suited Coral. She said the words she heard in his inaugural lecture haunted her through the years:

> In political activity, then, men sail a boundless and bottomless sea: there is neither harbour nor shelter nor floor for anchorage, neither starting-place nor appointed destination. The enterprise is to stay afloat on an even keel; the sea is both friend and enemy; and the seamanship consists of using the resources of a traditional manner of behaviour in order to make a friend of every hostile occasion.[19]

Throughout Coral's life, her intellectual anchor was international and strategic relations and crisis management. Her destination was our minds—and our hearts. And we found shelter in her kind words and wisdom.

A warm, engaging and humble spirit who gave of herself to others unselfishly, Coral imparted her knowledge without seeking validation in return. And, like some today and outside these walls, I came to understand the meaning of the word 'mentor'. Coral was compassionate, original, remarkable, astute and loyal, gracious, humble and independent. And the world is poorer for her no longer being here with us. Coral was for me—as for all those gathered here today—simply irreplaceable.

---

19 See Michael Oakeshott, 'Political Education: An Inaugural Lecture delivered at the London School of Economics and Political Science on 6 March 1951', Bowes & Bowes, Cambridge, 1951. Also see Michael Oakeshott, *Rationalism in Politics*, Methuen, London, 1962.

5. Coral Bell and Her Mark on Strategic Studies

Robert O'Neill

Coral Bell's death on 26 September 2012 has taken from our field one of Australia's most able specialists in strategic studies. This loss is felt both nationally and internationally by all who knew her and studied her works, not least because she remained intellectually active right until her passing at the age of eighty-nine. Her writing was clearly focused, she was interested in some of the most important international problems of her lifetime, and she had great gifts of wit and sparkle which have illuminated her publications over a fifty year period.

I first came to know Coral personally in the early 1970s, when she held a chair at the University of Sussex. Thereafter, through our membership of the International Institute for Strategic Studies (IISS), we had more regular contact, enabling me to see how highly regarded she was in Western Europe and North America. She became well known for her work on American foreign policy in the 1940s and 1950s, the nuclear weapons contest of the Cold War, and crisis management. I began to read her works in 1962, as a result of the publication of her second book, *Negotiation from Strength*.[1] This volume was a wonderfully powerful and illuminating analysis of US policy in the late 1940s and 1950s, and had much to teach any new scholar (such as myself) on the nature of the Cold War in the nuclear era. I first saw it soon after its publication in 1962, when browsing the shelves of Blackwells' Bookshop in Oxford during my time as a student there. Very soon I purchased my own copy. I also took heart from the discovery that an Australian scholar could achieve such a breakthrough on the home territory of many of the great names of our discipline.

Coral had come to adulthood during the Second World War, and knew from her own experience just how much was at stake when great powers went to war with modern weapons. The consequences of war were, of course, even more horrifying to think about in the 1950s when the opposing sides could use nuclear weapons on each other. Coral had become interested in weapons technology as a result of war work in the National Physics Laboratory in Sydney on de-magnetizing steel-hulled ships, known then as degaussing. She never forgot the experience of learning about the atomic bombing of Japan in 1945, and her fertile brain was able to imagine how the world would fare in an era

---

1   Coral Bell, *Negotiation from Strength: A Study in the Politics of Power,* Chatto & Windus, London, 1962, and Alfred A. Knopf, New York, 1963.

where these weapons had proliferated and become even more destructive than those of 1945. This experience coloured the whole of her intellectual life, as is made clear by the title of her unpublished memoir, 'A Preoccupation with Armageddon'.

Coral was fascinated by the importance of the challenges posed, and had the intellect and confidence to get to grips with them. In 1944 she opted for a career in diplomacy because she thought that it was the most interesting work available. She wanted to understand the nature of the problems presented by modern warfare, and have some influence on the development of national and international policies to deal with them. Initially the Department of External Affairs in Canberra gave her the stimulating assignment of analysing the Baruch Plan for the international control of nuclear weapons. However, as her conclusion to that study was that the Russians would kill it through refusal to participate, there did not seem much point in her continuing with that study. She moved on to study the Arab-Israeli problem, and then the Southeast Asian region. Given that she was also reading a mass of highly secret cables from London and Washington in those early years of the Cold War, she received an excellent grounding both in the complexities of these major international problems, and in the realities of power politics at the international level.

After six years, having seen that a diplomat, particularly a woman, was likely to be assigned minor responsibilities and a life of social tedium on the round of National Day receptions, cocktail parties and 'dips dinners', she decided in 1951 to pursue her professional interests through becoming an independent scholar of international relations. She had a lot to contribute to the policy-making deliberations of the Australian government, but not many people in the Department of External Affairs were prepared to listen to a young woman on these issues. She had not been impressed by being posted to Wellington. At least she had fared better in being admitted to Dr Evatt's Department of External Affairs than had Jill Ker Conway, later to be a celebrated author and academic, who in the late 1950s was turned down flat when she applied for an entry-level post in the same Department.

Coral knew how small was the group of Australian academics who specialised in international relations. Also she had a low opinion of several of them, so she decided to work in a wider arena, namely London, where she won a place as a graduate student at the London School of Economics (LSE). She arrived in time to experience the sea-change which occurred after Michael J Oakeshott replaced the deceased Harold Laski as Professor of Political Science. The Marxist-inspired values of Laski were replaced by a much more conservative flow of ideas and challenges from Oakeshott, which ran in parallel with other changes in dominant modes of thinking in other parts of the world. The Soviet Union in particular became much more the object of criticism and suspicion, and governments in many countries such as Britain and Australia turned from what Coral called a Fabian outlook towards something much more in harmony with the philosophies that Oakeshott espoused.

While she was at the LSE, Coral was strongly influenced by Martin Wight, whom she described as 'not only a friend and a colleague but the chief intellectual influence of my entire life'. She was also assisted by Geoffrey Goodwin who introduced her to the Royal Institute of International Affairs (RIIA, Chatham House). There she was appointed as rapporteur of a group of scholars who were assisting Goodwin in the production of a book on Britain and the United Nations.[2] Having worked in the United Nations Division of the Department of External Affairs in Canberra, Coral was well placed to make her own contributions to the group's thinking.

Soon afterwards she was appointed to assist Arnold Joseph Toynbee, Director of Studies at Chatham House, with the preparation of the *Survey of International Affairs for 1954*.[3] Toynbee had written the earlier volumes in this series himself, but after more than twenty years of such labours, he was keen to delegate the task to a younger person. After some initial testing of Coral's abilities, he selected her for the post. This appointment was important for Coral not only in terms of building her academic reputation but also as a necessary source of income while she was still a graduate student at the LSE. She distinguished herself in this, her first book, by lessening the usual emphasis of the series on European affairs and giving prominent treatment both to the French defeat at Dien Bien Phu, and to nuclear weapons and their implications for international politics.

Coral's post as rapporteur for the project on Britain and the United Nations gave her the opportunity to meet and get to know several rising British political and academic leaders, especially three who were to play major roles in founding the International Institute for Strategic Studies (IISS) in 1958: Denis Healey MP, Michael Howard and Alastair Buchan. She was impressed both by the intensity of their experience in the Second World War and by their belief that war had become too dangerous to be an acceptable way of solving international problems.

Her results at the LSE and Chatham House earned her the strength of reputation to compete successfully for a Lectureship in International Relations at the University of Manchester in 1956. This post gave her the opportunity to develop her ideas on how the US was managing the Cold War, and her doctoral thesis formed the basis of her second book, *Negotiation From Strength*. The central theme of her research became the development of Western policies which would maintain essential Western interests and values, while avoiding

---

2   See Geoffrey L Goodwin, *Britain and the United Nations*, National Studies on International Organization, Manhattan Publishing Company, New York, 1957.
3   See Coral Bell, *Survey of International Affairs for 1954*, Oxford University Press, London, 1956.

the need to go to war with nuclear weapons. To understand the bases of current Western security policies, she saw that it was necessary to undertake research and interviews in the United States. With the strong support of her department head at Manchester, Professor WJM ('Bill') Mackenzie, she won a Rockefeller Fellowship which gave her the necessary financial support, and some useful contacts, for her to spend several months in the United States in 1959. Coral certainly did not lack intellectual ambition and confidence, and by the time that she was aged thirty-six she was interviewing former senior US officials from Secretary of State Dean Acheson downwards, and she was applying her mind and powers of expression to the critical analysis of the most central elements of Western strategy in the early years of the Cold War.

One of the targets of her criticisms was the CIA-inspired operation to topple the Iranian nationalist leader, Dr Mossadegh, and put the young Shah back on his throne. Coral saw in this move a major encouragement for Islamic fundamentalists which would result in the overthrow of the Shah and the series of Ayatollah-led governments that Iran has had since then. She had become wary of United States administrations which exerted their economic and military power to re-shape other national societies in accordance with US preferences. This line of thought led her to oppose US military involvement in Vietnam. During her travels in the United States she became increasingly aware of the internal debate on policy towards Southeast Asia. Having administered Australian policies for Southeast Asia in the late 1940s, she knew a lot about that region and its conflicts, and could see how counter-productive a major American military effort there might be. On the other hand, as she examined US policy during the Korean War, she perceptively noted that the main American influence in that conflict was diplomatic rather than military. The military pressure applied by the Truman administration was to strengthen the UN Command's negotiating position rather than to achieve a military victory on the Korean Peninsula. At least the United States had learned from its Korean experience not to take Chinese passivity for granted in Vietnam. But this awareness did not enable the US to find a way to close off the vital supply links between China and North Vietnam on the 1960s. The two main rivals of the Korean War therefore faced each other for over a decade in Vietnam, while the North Vietnamese slowly built up their strength just as American public support for the conflict was declining.

During her time in the US in 1959, Coral also came to focus on nuclear weapons policy, and had the good fortune to interview Robert Oppenheimer, reputed to be 'the father of the atomic bomb' (with Enrico Fermi) and by then Director of the Institute of Advanced Studies at Princeton. Oppenheimer, who had been the object of political controversy in the United States for several years on account of his communist links in the 1930s, had been deprived of political power and influence, so the opportunity to be questioned rigorously by a young political scientist must have been stimulating for him, and he opened up, in the unguarded way that some senior US officials do when out of office. Oppenheimer was willing to discuss secret matters with Coral, and alerted her to the existence of the memorandum NSC-68, which was one of the main guidelines of American policy through the Cold War. Although she was not able to see a copy of this key policy statement on that visit, she soon learned enough about it through other interviews to have a reasonably detailed knowledge of its contents. Coral was impressed by its espousal of George Kennan's policy of containment of the Soviet Union, as she was by the friendship which existed between Kennan and Oppenheimer. She was learning at first hand of the fascinating debates in Washington on nuclear weapons policy and US–Soviet relations which were such a strong feature of the 1950s and 1960s. This was an excellent foundation for one of her main life-long fields of interest, as well as equipping her for a role in the debates on nuclear weapons policy which were the central element in the work of the International Institute for Strategic Studies in the 1950s and 1960s. It was all very stimulating for her research and writing on the policies of the great powers, and with this reserve of knowledge on which to draw, she was able to produce work at a high international standard and further enhance her rapidly growing reputation.

By the early 1960s Coral felt the pull of her homeland and successfully sought a post as a Senior Lecturer in Government at the University of Sydney, which she held from 1961 to 1965. She found the experience of being back in the midst of the Australian foreign policy debate disappointing, and even alienating. Australian foreign policy had been stuck in an orthodox conservative rut for over a decade, and while Coral was relatively conservative herself, she thought that the growing tensions between the United States and North Vietnam should be wound down and certainly not exploited as a justification for the United States and Australia to go to war in Vietnam. She became caught up in the discussions on Vietnam organised in Sydney by Dick Krygier and Owen Harries, two of the central figures in the production of *Quadrant*, then as now, a conservative journal which focused on culture and literature, but also covered foreign policy issues, among others.[4] Coral's perspective was that of an opponent of Soviet and Chinese attempts to gain more influence in world affairs, but who saw participation in a war in Vietnam as more likely to serve communist interests than those of the West. In putting forward these views, she had been greatly reinforced by her personal experience of the debate in the United States of the late 1950s and early 1960s.

---

4   See Coral Bell, 'The State of the Discipline: I.R.', *Quadrant*, vol. 12, no. 1, January–February 1968, pp. 79–84.; 'The Winning of the Cold War', *Quadrant*, vol. 34, no. 3, March 1990, pp. 13–24; 'The Future of Power in World Affairs', *Quadrant*, vol. 39, no. 9, September 1995, pp. 49–56; 'A Hard and Bitter Peace: The Cold War in Retrospect', *Quadrant*, vol. 40, no. 3, March 1996, pp. 18–22; 'World Out of Balance?', *Quadrant*, vol. 41, no. 7–8, 1997, pp. 35–40; and 'Washington and its Allies', *Quadrant*, vol. 41, no. 1–2, 1997, pp. 19–24.

The debate in Australia on Vietnam in the early 1960s had been influenced strongly by recent experience of The Malayan Emergency. It was further reinforced towards anti-communism by growing tensions with Indonesia which were to result in Australia's deployment of forces in Borneo to resist Soekarno's confrontation of Malaysia (1964–1965). Coral, having been out of Australia for most of the 1950s, saw things differently and did not want to plunge into a series of controversies with other experts who, on the whole, had similar views on the conduct of East–West relations in the broad, if not on Vietnam. As far as the Australian government was concerned, Menzies was very much in charge of foreign policy in the early 1960s. As she herself has written, 'Much more important, Australia seemed suddenly to be in a lonely place, internationally, diplomatically and strategically'. Coral's disapproval of government foreign policy views was fully mirrored by her low opinion of Labor leaders' views, especially those of Arthur Calwell, despite his opposition to the Vietnam War. Coral saw little hope of making an impression in policy-making circles with her views, so she turned her gaze back to the academic scene in Britain.

There she was soon successful, being offered a Readership in International Relations at the LSE, a senior post at one of the most prominent centres for the study of international relations in the world at that time. She enjoyed returning to the broader work in which she had been so heavily involved in the 1950s, and did well. She added to her reputation through her work for the IISS and Chatham House on nuclear weapons, American and NATO policies, and Western relations with the Soviet Union. In 1972 she was appointed to a Professorship at the University of Sussex, there working with her much-esteemed former colleague, Martin Wight.

After twelve years in Britain, Coral again felt the pull of home, drawn especially by the strength of the International Relations Department at The Australian National University (ANU) in Canberra. She had known JDB ('Bruce') Miller, the Head of the Department, in Britain in the 1950s, and while Coral was at the University of Sydney in the early 1960s, Bruce had relocated to ANU from the University of Leicester. Coral, however, in the 1960s regarded Canberra with no special favour, and preferred to return to London in 1965.

Much as she liked working in good British universities and living in London, Coral became increasingly uncomfortable at the growth of radicalism among the student body in the UK. Although she had remained opposed to the Vietnam War, her opinions on other major issues of the Cold War were on the conservative side, and she soon came under attack for some of her more 'realist' views of international affairs. Also administrative pressures were eroding the very collegial atmosphere that senior common room members in the UK enjoyed in the years before the Thatcher era. Thus, for several reasons, ANU seemed to

Coral in 1977 to be a better place in which to work than the UK. Also Canberra, no longer dominated by Menzies and his pro-British attitudes, seemed to Coral to be a much more interesting place to work in.

Another of the reasons for the change in Coral's attitudes towards Canberra had been Hedley Bull's work there from 1967 to 1977. They had known each other in London in the 1950s and 1960s, and had similar interests in power politics. Although Hedley had come and gone again before Coral made her move to Canberra in 1977, he had shown an ambitious scholar like Coral what could be achieved from ANU. Bruce had been keen to bring Coral to a senior, tenured post in the Department for some time, and she was appointed as a Senior Fellow in 1977. She worked in that capacity for the next eleven years until her formal retirement in 1988.

The ideological opposition that she had encountered was particularly galling to Coral because from the early 1960s she had been a profound sceptic about the ultimate worth of American and allied participation in the Vietnam War. She had studied the debate at first hand inside the United States in the late 1950s and early 1960s, and although the Vietnam War did not become a central part of her work, she did not fail to let everyone know that she was opposed to it. Having had to go to Vietnam myself as a member of the Australian Army, I did not share all her views on the conflict, particularly her willingness to allow the South Vietnamese to be ruled by a fairly dictatorial regime based in the North. But having seen how much of the US Army failed to learn from painful experience in Vietnam, it was not difficult for me to see the wisdom of Coral's overall evaluation as to how the war was likely to end. I learned a lot from her.

In 1977, when Hedley Bull left ANU for the Montague Burton Chair of International Relations at Oxford, a senior vacancy was thereby created in the ANU International Relations Department. Unfortunately it was not Hedley's chair, for ANU snaffled it back and left only a Senior Fellowship to be filled. But that was still an attractive position in terms of emoluments, research support and standing, and Coral was an obvious candidate. She was duly appointed and joined the Department for the following eleven years until she reached retiring age.

Coral was an expert organiser of interesting seminar series. She would build a series largely out of existing resources in terms of presenters, connected thematically to give PhD scholars and faculty members alike an opportunity to present their recent work. She was also an excellent seminar chair, keeping discussion focused on the most important issues, and moving along at a good speed. She could briskly terminate any self-indulgent monologues from other participants. Her seminar series continued to be in demand well after her official retirement, so she was appointed an Adjunct Fellow and continued to run discussions until well into the 1990s. She also maintained her international contacts by travelling, especially to the annual conferences of the International Institute for Strategic Studies, which gave me a good opportunity to catch up regularly with her views and activities in the post–1982 period. I well remember the warmth of Coral's greetings and how much I enjoyed her thoughts on what were likely to be the new issues to emerge in the forthcoming debates of this world-wide body of policy shapers, scholars and journalists.

During Coral's first five years at ANU, when I was the Head of the Strategic and Defence Studies Centre, she was a wise and supportive counsel, especially in university-political matters. She was a regular attendee at Centre seminars, discussion groups and conferences. One set of insights for which I shall always be grateful to her was her characterisation of the NATO alliance as 'always in disarray'. This appraisal has been truer over many years than many observers realise or will admit to. For most of its life in the twentieth century, NATO was good for one thing only: supporting the Germans against any Soviet conventional attack through Central or Northern Europe. For the rest it seemed to be largely an arena for complaints against the United States and debate about the need for making any commitment outside the 'NATO area'. For Australia there were some positive and some negative lessons from this experience of handling relations with the United States. For myself, as Director and then Chairman of the IISS, the wisdom of Coral's words on NATO was continually borne out through the 1980s and 1990s. I never forgot her characterisation.

For most of her professional academic life, Coral was primarily concerned with studying and analysing American methods of managing the alliance. While this focus had led her to oppose the war in Vietnam, she thought better of US policies in the field of arms control—a policy area that she held to be a very important way of stabilising the East-West relationship. Although Coral was regarded as a 'conservative realist', and even used that term about herself, she had her own very independent and well founded view of US policies and capabilities. Hence, like Owen Harries, another 'conservative realist', she was a strong critic of George W Bush's foreign and military policies. She could see how counterproductive Bush's illegal invasion of Iraq would be, and she became increasingly clear in her own mind that the US had lost 'sole super-power' status and was moving towards a world order in which power would be shared by several major states. Right until the last, Coral remained committed to this complex view of the world. She was certainly not a conservative in the American sense of the term.

I refer those interested in a more detailed summation of how Coral's thinking moved with, or ahead of, the times to an article she published in *American Review*, the journal of the United States Studies Centre of the University of

Sydney in 2009.[5] It is a forward-looking analysis of what President Obama had to do over the coming seven years of the two presidential terms that she gave him. While not an uncritical admirer of Barack Obama, Coral praised him for recognising that the world had undergone a 'profound, irreversible redistribution of power … that actually has far more to do with China and India than with the Europeans'. Obama's increased emphasis on the G20 was very much to his credit, and accorded with the real distribution of power in the world.

Coral developed this forward looking analysis on the basis of the historical record, particularly the experience of Europe in the nineteenth century, when its disputes were dealt with through the Concert of Powers mechanism, which had been set up to restore stability at the end of the Napoleonic Wars. With an experienced eye for the strengths and limitations of diplomacy, Coral advocated a broadening of this well-founded concept in order to help resolve the international problems of the twenty-first century. We are now five years further into the seven about which Coral was writing in 2009, and so far, so good. The world still has many problem areas and issues, from the proliferation of nuclear weapons to political instability within several key Islamic countries in the Middle East and South and Southeast Asia.

Her support for Obama's basic outlook on world affairs reveals a significant degree of change from the attitudes of a 'conservative realist' of the Cold War era who placed high value on authority and cohesion within alliance systems, nuclear weapons and arms control agreements. The causes of this change were two-fold: the rise of other powers within the international system, and the counter-productiveness of the policies of President George W Bush and his neo-con advisers. She was aware of the growing fragility of the international system and many of its second-level players, and the increasing leverage of non-state actors, who were anathema to someone who had learned about international relations from the perspective of a member of a well-run national diplomatic corps.

Coral brought together a capacity for anticipating political and strategic changes in the world, and a historical knowledge which enabled her to put forward ways and means for implementing new policies to deal with these changes and keep the world on an even keel. She was primarily interested in improving policy rather than in international relations theory. For the whole of her professional life she wrote clearly and comprehensibly on the major policy issues of the time—a demanding field in which to operate because there was so much competition. But she was better than most of the other analysts that she was up against. When she came to annual conferences of the International Institute for Strategic

---

5   Coral Bell, 'Seven Years to Get it Right', *American Review,* November 2009, http://americanreviewmag. com/stories/Seven-years-to-get-it-right, (accessed 11 November 2013).

Studies, she could always command a good audience of other participants, both in the formal sessions of the conference and the informal, over meals, coffee or cocktails. She had remarkable longevity as an expert analyst, serving as a model for us all of how to enjoy one's senior years without overdoing the commitment to professional work, while still maintaining a clearly visible position in the international panoply of distinguished scholars.

Her analytical legacy is a view of a world where US power and influence have been eroded through poorly thought-out policies and lack of understanding of the United States' own weaknesses in the first decade of this century. At the same time the capacities of China, Europe, Russia, and India have grown and they need to be taken more into account by the strongest power in the world, if it is not to be displaced by one or more of the others. For some, including myself, this view is a little too neat. It understates the likely influence of subnational groups, running to perhaps a few hundred persons each, some armed with weapons of mass destruction, and composed of young people willing to give their lives to kill Westerners. But Coral would respond to me that these subnational groups will lack the power of state governments and, with the right policies and military means, they could be ground down and eliminated individually. It was a merry discourse that we had in her apartment in Canberra on this topic three years ago. Who will be shown by events to be right?

Whatever our personal differences on matters of international policy, Coral was a splendid scholar and all of us who had the privilege of working with and learning from her, owe her a great debt for devotion to principles, intelligence, leadership and organising abilities. She had immense and accurate knowledge of international events and a warm nature. And she made an impressive climb to the high ground of international debate which is where most professional international relations analysts aspire to be. For all of us, regardless of nationality or gender, she has shown how to exert a wider impact in understanding our world.

Part 2: Understanding International Relations

6. The Interpretation of Power Politics: Coral Bell's International Thought

Ian Hall[1]

It is fair to say that Coral Bell remained somewhat sceptical about international relations theory throughout her long career. She could, at times, even be scathing about the subfield, calling it 'a very unimpressive growth', a plant that 'ought to be centrepiece and glory of the garden', but which—alas—had 'obstinately refused to put on more than a few inches in height, despite much watering, pruning, tilling, crooning over, and feeding with rare and expensive nutrients'.[2] She declared herself fully persuaded by Martin Wight's argument about the 'intractability of international experience' and the near-impossibility of theorising about such a challenging domain.[3] But none of this should distract attention from the fact that Bell had an international theory of her own, albeit one half-buried in her work, and rarely at the surface.

Bell's international theory was an old-fashioned kind, akin to that of the traditionalist realists and liberals of the first generation of theorists, who flourished before the behaviouralist revolution in the social sciences of the 1950s and all that came after. It sought to interpret the beliefs that shape policies and practices in international relations and to explain their evolution in historical perspective, with a particular focus on key agents and the ideas they espoused. She drew inspiration for her approach from many sources, but one was particularly important: her erstwhile mentor at the London School of Economics (LSE), Martin Wight.[4] She inherited from Wight a profound hostility to scientific approaches to the field and a staunch belief that studying international relations involved, as she put it, a 'meditation on history'.[5] In this, of course, she was not alone—various bits of the so-called 'English School of

1 I am very grateful to Desmond Ball, in particular, for asking me to write the chapter and talking to me about aspects of Bell's life and work, as well as to Renée Jeffery, Paul Keal and Brendan Taylor, for the various conversations about this piece.
2 Coral Bell, 'The State of the Discipline: I.R.', *Quadrant*, vol. 12, no. 1, January–February 1968, p. 82.
3 ibid., p. 82.
4 On Wight's ideas in general, see Ian Hall, *The International Thought of Martin Wight*, Palgrave, New York, 2006. Bell did graduate work under Wight's direction at the London School of Economics in the early 1950s. He later helped appoint her to the Professorship of International Relations at Sussex, where Wight served as Professor of History and Dean of European Studies from 1961 until his untimely death in 1972.
5 Bell, 'The State of the Discipline', p.83. Wight used the same phrase in unpublished papers. See, for example, 'History and the Study of International Relations', no date, but probably mid–1950s, Wight MS 112, British Library of Political and Economic Sciences, p. 1.

International Relations' have put this argument since Wight suggested it in the 1950s and Hedley Bull popularised it in the 1960s and 1970s.[6] Bell departed from Wight and from his followers, however, in one important aspect: unlike them, she had no time for what she called the 'metaphysics of history'.[7]

Her attachment to the past and her dislike of the 'metaphysics of history', together with an innate scepticism, helped make Bell a conservative. Her fascination for power—or, rather, for the ways in which power is wielded in international relations—made her a realist, of sorts. But the label 'conservative realist' makes Bell sound theoretically unsophisticated—except to the occasional admirer[8]—and her international thought was not. So this chapter sets that label aside, not so much because it is inaccurate but because it is unhelpful in the task at hand. It argues instead that Bell advanced what might best be called an agent-centred interpretive theory of international relations. This might not be the most elegant description—and Bell would probably have disliked it—but it is, the chapter contends, the most revealing about her international thought.

Foundations

Bell came to the study of international relations as many of her generation of British and Australian scholars did, through the study of history, and especially through the work of good history teachers. In a short memoir, she recalled how her interest in the past and its relationship to the present was kindled at both primary school and Sydney Girls High. At the latter, she noted, she was 'encouraged ... to see the world of current events as history just waiting to be written' and asked to write it, producing an essay on the Munich Crisis of 1938 in its immediate aftermath.[9] Bell nurtured these interests at the University of Sydney, studying history as well as literature, economics and philosophy,

---

6 On the English school in general, see Tim Dunne, *Inventing International Society: A History of the English School*, Macmillan, Basingstoke, 1997; and on Bull's views, see especially his 'International Theory: A Case for a Classical Approach', *World Politics*, vol. 18, no. 3, 1966, pp. 361–377. Richard Devetak rightly acknowledges Bell's close relationship with the early English school in his 'An Australian Outlook on International Affairs? The Evolution of International Relations Theory in Australia', *Australian Journal of Politics and History*, vol. 55, no. 3, 2009, p. 349.

7 Bell, 'The State of the Discipline', p. 84. For English school ventures into that area, see inter alia Martin Wight, 'The Church, Russia and the West', *Ecumenical Review*, vol.1, no. 1, 1948, pp. 25–45, Herbert Butterfield, *History and Human Relations*, Collins, London, 1951; and Peter Savigear, 'International Relations and the Philosophy of History', in Michael Donelan (ed), *The Reason of States: A Study in International Political Theory*, Allen & Unwin, London, 1978, pp. 195–205.

8 Robert O'Neill observes that Bell sometimes used this phrase to describe herself, but also finds it unhelpful—see his obituary 'Coral Bell AO 1923–2012: A balanced, independent, realist-minded scholar of world politics', *The Interpreter*, Lowy Institute for International Policy, 3 October 2012. http://www.lowyinterpreter.org/post/2012/10/03/Coral-Bell-AO-1923-2012-a-balanced-independent-realist-minded-scholar-of-world-politics.aspx (accessed 2 August 2013).

9 Coral Bell, 'A Preoccupation with Armageddon', unpublished memoir, Canberra, 2012, p. 2.

taking full advantage of a broad curriculum and an impressive faculty, including the great empiricist philosopher, John Anderson, who also taught Hedley Bull.[10] These studies served Bell well, helping her to secure the position in the Department of External Affairs she held from 1945 to 1951. In turn, her government work provided invaluable—and, if her memoir is any guide, eye-opening[11]—experience of the making of foreign policy and the practice of diplomacy.

Bell's enduring interest in the past and her interest in the practices of international relations no doubt predisposed her to Wight, whom she later called 'the chief intellectual influence of my entire life', and his approach to the field.[12] In 1951, when Bell resigned from External Affairs and applied for graduate studies at the LSE, Wight was a relatively minor figure in the nascent but tiny field of International Relations, and a man with a somewhat unusual background. Born in 1913 into a relatively prosperous middle-class family, Wight read Modern History at Hertford College, Oxford in the tumultuous early 1930s. He won a First but also engaged in university politics, becoming known as a passionate defender of the League of Nations at a time when many were starting to question its efficacy. Wight abandoned that cause soon after leaving Oxford, during the Abyssinian crisis of 1935–36, turning instead to Christian pacifism and the Reverend 'Dick' Sheppard's 'Peace Pledge Union' (PPU). At around the same time, Wight began to further his professional interest in international relations, securing a temporary post at Chatham House, where he worked closely with its Director of Studies, Arnold J Toynbee, the author of the *Survey of International Affairs* and *A Study of History*.[13] After three years or so, Wight moved on again, this time to become a History Master at Haileybury School, but he was forced to give up this post in 1940 after a failed application to register as a conscientious objector. He passed the remainder of the war back at Oxford, working (unhappily) with Margery Perham on British colonial constitutions. In 1945, he escaped Oxford and Perham to travel to the United States and spend a year as *The Observer* newspaper's United Nations

---

10   On Anderson and Bull, see Renée Jeffery, 'Australian Realism and International Relations: John Anderson and Hedley Bull on Ethics, Religion and Society', *International Politics*, vol. 45, no. 1, 2008, pp. 52–71.

11   See especially Bell, 'A Preoccupation with Armageddon', pp. 5–10.

12   ibid., p. 13.

13   Arnold J Toynbee, *Survey of International Affairs*, various vols., Royal Institute of International Affairs and Oxford University Press, London, 1924–58; and *A Study of History*, 12 vols., Oxford University Press, London, 1934–61.

correspondent. After another brief stint at Chatham House, Wight finally ended up at the LSE, where the idiosyncratic head of the Department of International Relations, Charles Manning,[14] appointed him to a Readership in 1949.[15]

Wight's early scholarly achievements were few, but what he had published was well-regarded. The highlight was a seventy page pamphlet produced for Chatham House, *Power Politics* (1946),[16] which displayed Wight's extraordinary historical range as well as his analytical acuity and moral concern. Other projects, however, distracted him from making further significant contributions to the field. By the time Bell met Wight in 1951, Wight's only other substantial works of scholarship were three reference works on colonial constitutions and four brilliant but over-wrought essays in a forthcoming volume of the Chatham House *Survey of International Affairs* covering the war-years.[17] His journalism, reviewing and extensive reading unquestionably slowed Wight's productivity, but so did two other things: his suspicion about the ways in which international relations was being approached, at that time, as an academic discipline and his exacting approach to the study of world politics.

Wight was sceptical about international relations when he accepted his Readership in 1949 and he was just as sceptical when he resigned it twelve years later, to take up a Chair in History. He disliked the social sciences in general, for what might today be considered peculiar reasons—he thought them dehumanising, but also a sign of a neo-pagan return to cyclic views of human destiny once banished by Christian historiography.[18] His religious beliefs—he was a devout but intellectual Anglican—prevented him accepting that history could repeat itself, and thus prevented him from accepting that general 'laws' about social life could ever be determined. Only philosophy, literature and history were capable of capturing truths about human societies, Wight argued, and only these disciplines should underpin political thought and practice.[19] In

---

14   On Manning, see Hidemi Suganami, 'C. A. W. Manning and the study of international relations', *Review of International Studies*, vol. 27, no. 1, 2001, pp. 91–107; and David Long, 'C. A. W. Manning and the discipline of international relations', *The Round Table*, vol. 95, no. 378, 2005, pp. 77–96, as well as Manning's own *The Nature of International Society*, Macmillan, London, 1962.

15   On these various details of Wight's early career and thought, see Hall, *International Thought of Martin Wight*, pp. 4–8.

16   Martin Wight, *Power Politics*, Looking Forward Pamphlet no. 8, Royal Institute of International Affairs, London, 1946.

17   See Martin Wight, *The Development of the Legislative Council, 1606-1945*, Faber & Faber, London, 1946; *The Gold Coast Legislative Council*, Faber & Faber, London, 1947; and *British Colonial Constitutions 1947*, Clarendon, Oxford, 1952; as well as his essays on 'Spain and 'Portugal', 'Switzerland, The Low Countries, and Scandinavia', 'Eastern Europe', 'Germany', and 'The Balance of Power', in AJ Toynbee and FT Ashton-Gwatkin (eds), *Survey of International Affairs 1939–1946: The World in March 1939*, Oxford University Press, London, 1952, pp. 138–150, pp. 151–165, pp. 206–292, pp. 293–365 and pp. 508–532.

18   See especially Martin Wight, 'History and Judgment: Butterfield, Niebuhr and the Technical History', *The Frontier: A Christian Commentary on the Common Life*, *v*ol. 1, no. 8, 1950, p. 306.

19   As Wight wrote to his friend and erstwhile colleague at the LSE, Elie Kedourie, 'the teaching of International Relations … convinced me that the only subjects which ought to be taught were philosophy, literature and history' (Wight to Kedourie, 21 November 1961, *Wight MS* 233 3/9, British Library of Political and Economic Sciences, London).

his mind, the new social sciences were implicated in some way with not merely the secularisation of the West, which he lamented, but also the rise of new and more extreme forms of tyranny to any that had existed in the past.[20]

These beliefs conditioned Wight's approach to international relations. He was convinced that world politics required serious study, but unconvinced by the approaches used and the findings generated since the first chairs in the discipline were founded in the 1920s. Just after he first arrived at the LSE he proposed that the subject should have two poles: contemporary history and what he called, uncomfortably, but with hints of necessary deference to Manning's preferences, the 'Sociology of the International Community'. He rejected the objections of some professional historians to the study of contemporary history as palpably silly—they argued that it could not be written for lack of available sources, by which they meant official archives; Wight objected by saying—rightly— that medievalists work with far less. Some of the greatest history, he noted, was contemporary history: think of Thucydides, Clarendon or Churchill. But Wight argued that students of the field could not stop at contemporary history: they needed also to explore the relationships between 'powers', especially the 'certain kinds of habitual behaviour' which have 'crystallised in diplomacy'.[21]

How might this be done? Wight had been trained as a historian in the early 1930s, and at Oxford, where the History Faculty was notoriously conservative. In Cambridge, at the same time, historians had long been concerned with general and thematic history, and were then experimenting further, with social and economic history, with Marxist and sociological modes of analysis, and with the histories of science and medicine. At Oxford, however, the syllabus remained dominated by the political (primarily constitutional) history of England, studied by exhaustive investigation of mainly short periods. The principal concerns were ideas and institutions: the study of the changing ideas that informed the evolving institutions of English government.

Wight disliked the Oxford curriculum intensely, as he later recalled,[22] but never fully escaped it. He shared Toynbee's belief that human societies only made sense to the observer if they were approached as wholes, but struggled to reconcile this belief in 'holism' with his continued insistence that the past must still be studied by the meticulous examination of primary sources.[23] Understandably, this requirement placed too great a burden on Wight's own shoulders—he found it impossible to meet his own standards of scholarship and his output suffered as a consequence. He was able, however, to transmit some

---

20 See Hall, *International Thought of Martin Wight*, especially pp.6 5–85 (on 'The Crisis of Modern Politics').
21 Martin Wight, 'What is International Relations?' (1950), *Wight MS* 112, p. 17.
22 Martin Wight, 'Devising a History Syllabus', talk given at Reading, 28 February 1963, *Wight MS* 50.
23 On Wight's relationship with Toynbee's thought, see Ian Hall, 'Challenge and Response: The Lasting Engagement of Arnold J Toynbee and Martin Wight', *International Relations*, vol. 17, no. 3, 2003, pp. 389–404.

elements of what he had inherited as an Oxford historian to his students. Above all, there was the insistence that politics is best explained in terms of ideas and institutions—specifically, the beliefs of agents and what we would now call the 'norms' of behaviour those beliefs generated—and best studied by looking at what politicians, diplomats, lawyers and other practitioners, say about those ideas and institutions.

This was Wight's vision of the study of international relations that Bell encountered in 1951 and that she carried forward, albeit with her own modifications. It combined the study of contemporary history and the institutions of international society—not the formal institutions, like the United Nations, but the informal ones that had arisen over time, like war or diplomacy, for managing the relations of political communities. It entailed the rigorous examination of the beliefs of decision-makers, the ways in which these beliefs shaped their perceptions of their circumstances, and manner in which these beliefs and perceptions shaped their changing practices. It was, in other words, an 'interpretive' approach to international theory which puts the beliefs of policy-actors and the traditions of thought that shape those beliefs centre-stage, as explanations for what occurs in international relations. It rejects the idea that systems and structures determine events and emphasises agency, contingency and contestability.[24]

Beliefs, Conventions and Crises

Under Wight's supervision, Bell's graduate work was an apprenticeship in this interpretive approach to international relations. She was set a project that involved the examination of a belief or set of beliefs and their effect on international practice in contemporary world politics: in her particular case, the idea of 'containment' and the ways in which it was translated into policy. Others who worked with Wight at around the same time were set similar tasks. For Hedley Bull, who arrived at the LSE as an Assistant Lecturer in 1955, soon after Bell's departure for Manchester, and began a PhD there under Wight's direction, it involved various aspects of Labour Party internationalism.[25] For others, like Peter Lyon, it was 'neutralism' and 'nonalignment'.[26]

For most of the first half of the 1950s, Bell balanced this work on containment at the LSE with other commitments at Chatham House, where she was employed

---

24   For further explorations of the interpretive approach, see Mark Bevir, Oliver Daddow and Ian Hall, 'Introduction: Interpreting British Foreign Policy', *British Journal of Politics and International Relations*, vol. 15, no. 2, 2013, pp. 163–174.

25   See Robert Ayson, *Hedley Bull and the Accommodation of Power*, Palgrave MacMillan, Basingstoke, 2012.

26   Peter Lyons, *Neutralism*, Leicester University Press, Leicester, 1963.

as a research officer. Her duties included aiding the production of key projects, including Geoffrey Goodwin's ponderous *Britain and the United Nations* (1957), but she was also able to make a more substantial contribution of her own: the *Survey of International Affairs for 1954* (1956).[27] Bell recalls in her memoir that Chatham House provided the invaluable opportunity to meet and to speak to scholars and policy-makers in a relatively informal setting. But it also provided much-needed resources for the writing of contemporary history in the 1950s, not least the scrupulously-maintained press-cuttings archive that Toynbee had built up since the 1920s, which included material from newspapers and wire services across the world. Toynbee's inter-war *Surveys* were greatly dependent on these resources; Bell's volume is too. Apart from personal interactions with politicians and diplomats, these cuttings were the core source material of contemporary history until at least the latter part of the 1960s.

Bell used these kinds of materials not merely to determine factual information but also to gain insight into the beliefs of practitioners, a task that Wight insisted was crucial to the proper study of international relations. Beliefs dominate Bell's first major book, *Negotiation from Strength* (1962),[28] which grew out of her graduate studies at the LSE. Her principal concern in the book is to tell the story of the rise and fall of a policy concept, 'negotiation from strength', which emerged in American foreign policy circles in 1950 as a possible alternative to 'containment'. But Bell also had another concern: to explore '[w]hat makes "an effective decision"'. 'How many people', she asked, 'have to feel what degree of conviction to turn aspiration into intention and intention into actual policy?'.[29] And there were other issues too. Bell was interested not just in the failure of a concept to be translated into an effective policy, but also the failure of that concept to disappear once its initial shortcoming had been detected.

These were big questions and *Negotiation from Strength*—arguably Bell's best book—delivered some intriguing answers. It shows how containment was replaced by a Western (mainly American) aspiration to be able to 'negotiate from strength' was related not just to changes in key personnel—principally from George Kennan to Paul Nitze, and from Harry Truman to John Foster Dulles—but to the relative popularity of differing accounts of Soviet strategy and diplomacy. Proponents of containment, Bell notes, believed that the 'power struggle' between the US and USSR would only end with domestic political change within the Soviet Union; proponents of negotiation from strength

---

27   See Geoffrey Goodwin, *Britain and the United Nations*, Royal Institute of International Affairs and Oxford University Press, London, 1957; and Coral Bell, *Survey of International Affairs for 1954*, Royal Institute of International Affairs and Oxford University Press, London, 1956.

28   Coral Bell, *Negotiation Negotiation from Strength: A Study in the Politics of Power*, Chatto & Windus, London, 1962, and Alfred A. Knopf, New York, 1963.

29   ibid., p. 12.

assumed, by contrast, that 'diplomatic adjustment' was possible.[30] During the course of the 1950s, she demonstrates, negotiation from strength came to replace containment as the dominant policy concept for the West, especially for American decision-makers. This occurred despite the hostility of John Foster Dulles, in particular, to diplomacy in general and to negotiation with the USSR in particular.[31]

Bell's book traces this story in minute detail and considerable insight into the beliefs of the key figures involved—without, it should be noted, any access to official documents. Her pen-portrait of Dulles and what she calls his 'theory of international politics' is especially perceptive and characteristically unemotive: she picks through his published works, interviews and profiles, and draws upon backgrounding interviews she carried out in Washington to provide a dispassionate assessment of his motives and his strategy.[32] Bell argues that despite Dulles' position and extraordinary energy, he was overtaken by demands for negotiation as he worked to build American and allied strength. These came from Winston Churchill and indeed from the Soviets themselves, and from the general public. But the most powerful part of the book, arguably, is Bell's assessment of the perceptions of the participants in the negotiations, especially how they miscalculated and misunderstood their adversaries and failed to achieve any kind of deal.[33]

What, then, did Bell think we might learn from the rise and fall of negotiation from strength? In the conclusion, she reflected:

> [I]t may be regarded … as chiefly an illustration of how two competing alliances may be bound to the policy-purposes of their most vulnerable members, or … as an illustration of the progress of a policy through stages of ambition, distraction, approximation and supersession, as a study in cross-purposes and the political uses of illusion, an example of how wide the gap may be between declared policy and what is actually done, and of how much more important in politics than intention is what Fisher called the play of the contingent and the unforeseen.[34]

This is a distinctively 'interpretivist' passage and a subtle one. Bell suggested that negotiation from strength might be regarded as little more than an 'official myth' or a 'harmless necessary public-relations-man's phrase'—a kind of noble lie that comforts democratic electorates but means little.[35] But to dismiss it that way would be to ignore the ways in which the concept clearly shaped

---

30   ibid., p. 29.
31   ibid., pp. 67–76.
32   See especially ibid., pp. 93–94.
33   ibid., pp. 112–125.
34   ibid., p. 188.
35   ibid., p. 189.

policy, albeit a failed one, and shaped expectations of what might be possible and what might eventuate. As Bell argued later, she was convinced that '[i]nternational politics proceeds essentially on nothing more substantial than a set of expectations: expectations as to where power will prove to be and how it will be used'.[36]

Bell's subsequent work—with the major exception of *The Diplomacy of Détente*, which concentrates on the beliefs and behaviour of one man above all: Henry Kissinger[37]—focussed less on beliefs and more on what she called 'conventions'. We might call them social institutions, perhaps laws (in a social scientific sense), or even just norms. What Bell meant by conventions was 'just what it conveys in ordinary parlance: expected or understood signals (as in the conventions of bridge), or rules of behaviour with no particular moral or legal backing, sanctioned chiefly by prudence and custom, and stemming from a particular society'.[38] Here again, Bell moved in a Wightean universe, but in parts Wight himself neglected. He had argued that international society was defined and ordered by its 'institutions'—not formal institutions, like the UN, but informal bundles of beliefs, expectations, rules and indeed conventions of behaviour. Borrowing from contemporary social anthropology, consciously or not, Wight cast war, diplomacy, international law, great powers and the balance of powers as social 'institutions' in which there were assumptions, acceptances and anticipations of particular kinds of behaviour by practitioners.[39]

Bell narrowed her concerns merely to conventions and especially to what she termed, in the book of the same name, *The Conventions of Crisis* (1971).[40] Her interest was in the evolving conventions that existed during crises— expectations around behaviour and conduct—focussing attention once more upon the beliefs of practitioners as the motive forces of international relations. Crisis management, she argued, is 'learned behaviour' which may or may not be 'institutionalised'—by which she meant learned, taught and re-learned within communities of practitioners.[41] The conventions that might be used, learned and taught varied: they could be forms of signalling, some crude and some highly subtle, military, economic, political or diplomatic, or certain techniques,

---

36 Coral Bell, 'Local Threats and the Central Balance', in her edited *Academic Studies and International Politics: Papers of a Conference held at the Australian National University, June 1981*, Canberra Studies in World Affairs, The Australian National University, no. 6, 1982, p. 151.

37 Coral Bell, *The Diplomacy of Détente: The Kissinger Era*, Martin Robertson, London, 1977.

38 Coral Bell, 'Crisis Diplomacy', in Laurence Martin, ed., *Strategic Thought in a Nuclear Age*, Heinemann, 1979, London, p. 158.

39 See especially Wight's *Power Politics*.

40 Coral Bell, *The Conventions of Crisis: A Study in Diplomatic Management*, Oxford University Press for the Royal Institute of International Affairs, London and New York, 1971.

41 ibid., p. 25.

like the 'creative use of ambiguity'.[42] And crucially, in Bell's world, they come into play when self-consciously and deliberately selected by individual agents confronted with changing sets of circumstances.

In this way, Bell succeeded in developing Wight's interpretive approach, with its emphasis on agents and beliefs, but succeeded not just in describing the emergence of concepts and policies, but also in explaining significant changes in the everyday practices of the society of states. Other thinkers influenced by the early English School struggled to get this balance right. Bull, for example, in his *The Anarchical Society*, never got into sufficient detail to really explain how that society and its institutions were changing and why.[43] Bell's dogged focus on crisis management, by contrast, tells us a great deal more about what is evolving and what is perennial, giving her the platform for later works, like *A World Out of Balance*,[44] that take the 'long view' of contemporary events and generate important arguments about the drivers of change in international relations.

Conclusion

Bell's other perennial concern—apart from conventions—was 'power politics' or, more precisely, because that term has become synonymous with international relations, the politics of power. She was concerned with how power was conceived and especially how it was used, principally by great powers. But for Bell 'power' did not mean the material capabilities of actors. It was a much more complex concept. Power was something perceived or misperceived, calculated or miscalculated, not innate in a set of resources or weapons. Power was relational: it implied to Bell the capacity of one party to influence or even control the actions of others. Power could be wielded in crude ways, by making military threats or imposing economic sanctions, by forcing others to bend to one's will. But equally power could consist of the ability to seize and hold an agenda, to articulate a set of ideas and thereby to force others to justify or even modify their behaviour. Power might flow from a concerted effort to utilise an institution or to mobilise opinion—something which even those who lack material military or economic power can do.

One of Bell's earliest articles dealt with these kinds of uses of power by the hitherto powerless. Her 'The United Nations and the West' (1953), published in the Chatham House journal *International Affairs*, bears like her other work of

---

42   ibid., p. 74.
43   Hedley Bull, *The Anarchical Society: A Study of Order in World Politics*, 2nd edn, Macmillan, London, 1995.
44   Coral Bell, *A World Out of Balance: American Ascendancy and International Politics in the 21st Century*, Longueville Books, Double Bay, 2003.

that period the distinct signs of the influence of Wight in its composition and its message,[45] but it is also revealing about Bell's own views. She opens with the observation—commonplace in British international thought in the immediate post-war years—that the Second World War and its aftermath had brought about the 'contraction of Europe' after two hundred years of expansion and the 'eclipse of Europe in Power-terms' not just by the United States and the Soviet Union, but by anti-colonial forces.[46] The latter, Bell acknowledged, might be relatively weak in material terms, but they are irresistible politically:

> Political control rests on elements of consent and coercion, and the belief that the controlling Power can exert force of a decisive kind tends to reduce to the minimum the amount actually needed. Conversely, where doubt is thrown upon the effective power available to the controlling nations, as in the case of the defeat of the European Powers in South East Asia by Japan, forces inimical to that control are encouraged, and the re-imposition of authority is rendered difficult or impossible.[47]

Bell's concern in this article, however, was not so much with challenges to European authority on what used to be called the colonial periphery, but with the ways in which those 'forces inimical to control' mobilised themselves at the UN to build and project power.

Bell's power politics was a politics with agency where the materially-rich did not, as many other realists might argue, necessarily prevail. International politics were to her an arena in which agents manoeuvred, making good or bad use of both the intellectual and material resources they had at their disposal. For that reason, the beliefs of agents mattered, because they informed the ways in which they approached predicaments, deployed what resources they had at their disposal, and shaped policies to achieve their objectives. What Bell presented in her international thought, in other words, was a vision of international relations that was both human and humane.

---

45   For a point of comparison, see Martin Wight's 'The Power Struggle at the United Nations', *Proceedings of the Institute of World Affairs*, 33rd session, University of Southern California, Los Angeles, 1956, pp. 247–259.
46   Coral Bell, 'The United Nations and the West', *International Affairs*, vol. 29, no. 4, 1953, pp. 464–465.
47   ibid., p. 465.

7. The Importance of Being Coral Bell[1]

JDB Miller

Declaring one's interest is often necessary, very much in this case. I have known and admired Coral Bell for fifty years, ever since she and I were tutoring students in International Relations at the London School of Economics (LSE). She has since become the most respected and prolific of Australians in this field, and remains an acute analyst of what happens in the world, especially in terms of conflict and alliances.

Having graduated from the University of Sydney, she entered the Australian Diplomatic Service. After some time abroad, she evidently decided to enter academic life, and proceeded to the LSE to do postgraduate work. There she came under the influence of Martin Wight and became a colleague of Hedley Bull. Even though I would personally regard it as to some extent a barren time because of the tenure of Professor Charles Manning as Head of Affairs, there was no doubt of the effect of Wight's personality and his awareness of the international system: he was an inspiration to all who knew him. When, years later, he told me that, when asked to recommend someone for the Chair of International Relations at Sussex University, he could only hesitate between two Australians, Coral Bell and Hedley Bull. Coral took the job.

The Sussex Department turned out to be an unhappy place; after some time, Coral thought of returning to Australia. Hedley and I, learning of this, were delighted to lure her to the Department of International Relations in the Research School of Pacific Studies at The Australian National University (ANU), of which we were joint heads. Here she continued her published work, and contributed to both the Department and the Strategic and Defence Studies Centre. She joined Hedley, Robert O'Neill, TB Millar and myself as a Fellow of the Academy of the Social Sciences in Australia. She continues to produce: the ANU Library lists thirty books she has either written (the majority), edited, or contributed to (the smallest category). They cover the world situation, Australian foreign policy, and particularly American policy under a succession of presidents.

The work displays great clarity with an absence of jargon, much practicality and historical sense, and a full awareness of the problems of high-level diplomacy,

---

1   This is a revised version of an article previously published by Taylor & Francis Ltd., as: JDB Miller, 'The Importance of Being Coral Bell', *Australian Journal of International Affairs*, vol. 59, no. 3, September 2005, pp. 261–263; and has been reprinted by permission of the publisher.

as, for example, in her studies of John Foster Dulles and Henry Kissinger. It is not surprising that she has been widely acknowledged in Britain and the US for the depth and range of her thinking.

Though her numerous books on the international situation are all important, it seems to me that Coral Bell's main interest and considerable achievement lie in the foreign policy of the US, a power which has been dominant (but not always successful) in the international system, and which she knows intimately through personal contact and frequent visits. For the purposes of this treatment I shall concentrate on a single article, hoping to indicate her methods and her insight into how the US goes about its activities, and why. The article is 'American Policy in the Third World'.[2]

Bell makes it clear that the US is an 'intensely plural society'—a matter not sufficiently recognised in much Australian discussion of the country, which tends to concentrate on the east and west coasts and ignores the mid-west and south and the social make-up. She discerns two earlier strands in US policy towards the Caribbean and Latin America, those identified with Theodore Roosevelt's aggressive 'backyard' policy, in which the US pushed the Monroe Doctrine to extremes, and the 'good neighbour' policy of Franklin Roosevelt, which, along with private efforts, emphasised humanitarian and friendly connections with the often unruly neighbours to the south.

Her point in recalling this history is that these two traditions persist: even in such apparently belligerent regimes as those of Richard Nixon and Ronald Reagan, one can see both strands at work. She sees them extend in later years, including the present, from the western hemisphere to the Third World at large—though she does not accept the notion that there is a unified Third World: it is individual Third World countries, especially in the Middle East, that she has in mind.

Out of this matrix of earlier and recent themes she sees two approaches to US foreign policy. On the one hand,

> American official spokesmen ... desire and promote change (in the 'right' direction, admittedly), citing the official Wilsonian progressive notions of human rights and national self-determination, and making a case for linking these political desiderata to economic policies allowing reasonable play to the forces of the market.

Bell sees these attitudes as having been largely dominant in recent times, but with an underlay of attitudes of the second strand, preserved in the bureaucracy,

---

2   See Coral Bell, 'American Policy in the Third World' in Robert O'Neill and RJ Vincent, (eds), *The West and the Third World*, Macmillan, London, 1990, pp. 51–66.

and reflected in the fact that US public opinion, especially liberal-democratic opinion, maintained an authentic humanitarian concern for the welfare of Third World peoples in general, and that strand of public feeling was quite articulate, and also quite able to bring pressure to bear on Washington policy-makers, even in the days of the 'Reagan Doctrine', as witness Congressional recalcitrance on Nicaragua.

She sees 'a large gap between operational and declaratory policies, what the President [Reagan] did and what he said.' Perhaps it will be the same with all administrations, the two strands/traditions coinciding and clashing in varying degrees. Bell sums it up:

> The Reagan Administration's decision-making process (if that is not too charitable a term) seems even more dispersed and incoherent than has been the case for most American administrations. And nowhere was that more true than on Third World issues. Thus the inherent pluralism of American society was often expressed in what seemed a confused and confusing multiplicity of attitudes and policies.

Of course, much has changed since 11 September 2001 and the re-election of President George W Bush. Yet Bell's analysis, based on history and shrewd and penetrating as it is, remains a reliable guide to much of how American policy proceeds. There is much more to ponder in the realism of her other writings: she has brought a practical and sophisticated analysis to the study of the international system and Australia's reaction to it. She continues to do so. That is the importance of Coral Bell.

8. Coral Bell and the Classical Realist Tradition[1]

James L Richardson

Like JDB Miller, I have known Coral Bell for half a century, having met her in London in 1955-56—I an intending graduate student, she already an established scholar at Chatham House. Later our paths crossed quite frequently, but we were direct colleagues only for a few years in the 1980s, in the Department of International Relations at The Australian National University.

Her contributions to international relations are multifaceted, but I shall focus on three of her books on American foreign policy and Cold War diplomacy— each of them a significant and timely input into the scholarly discussion of the burning issues of the day. (It is easily forgotten how intense were some of the concerns, and how fierce some of the debates, in those years). The books in question—*Negotiation from Strength* (1963), *The Conventions of Crisis* (1971) and *The Diplomacy of Detente* (1977)—influenced my understanding of the issues at the time, when I was working on closely related topics. Returning to them, one is not only reminded of old debates but also rewarded with new insights.[2]

Negotiation from Strength offers a sparkling commentary on the 1950s: the decade during which the Cold War in Europe hardened into a rigid confrontation between two heavily armed military blocs, seemingly in perpetuity. At first sight, the diplomatic formula which provides the book's title offered little more than a device for indefinitely deferring unwanted negotiations, but Bell shows that, on the contrary, the varied uses of the formula can serve to illuminate the potentialities for a more imaginative Western diplomacy during those years, and the reasons why this was not attempted. The reader gains a heightened sense of choices forgone and an appreciation of the qualities of key decision-makers—of Winston Churchill's eagerness to explore potential openings for diplomacy, Dean Acheson's scepticism and John Foster Dulles's stubborn belief in the dangers attending any negotiation.

She does not, in the manner of George Kennan's advocacy of disengagement, argue for a particular course of action, but more subtly counters the familiar

---

1   This is a revised version of an article previously published by Taylor & Francis Ltd., as: James L Richardson, 'Coral Bell and the classical realist tradition', *Australian Journal of International Affairs,* vol. 59, no. 3, September 2005, pp. 265–268; and has been reprinted by permission of the publisher.

2   See Coral Bell, *Negotiation from Strength: A Study in the Politics of Power,* Alfred A. Knopf, New York, 1963; *The Conventions of Crisis: A Study in Diplomatic Management,* Oxford University Press, Oxford, 1971; and *TheDiplomacy of Detente: The Kissinger Era,* Martin Robertson, London, 1977.

apprehensions of the risks of negotiation with the unfamiliar thesis of the costs of indefinitely postponing it. Her thesis is that in the pursuit of absolute military strength the Western leaders lost sight of the relative overall strength of their position in the early to mid–1950s. By the early 1960s, a skilful Soviet diplomatic offensive had narrowed the agenda to the preservation, or otherwise, of the special status of West Berlin. For contemporaries this was a highly challenging interpretation of the central Cold War issues. For later scholars it offers many illuminating insights: into the (often unfortunate) interplay of domestic and external 'imperatives'; the role of key decision-makers (the sketch of Dulles has not been improved upon); and the relentless priority accorded to the military build-up, but also the facile claims associated with it. For this reader, the multiplicity of reasons for American policy-makers' subordinating diplomatic to narrowly conceived military considerations remains of particular interest.

This is not a criticism that can be made of Henry Kissinger, whose diplomacy is examined in *The Diplomacy of Detente*. Indeed, although Bell does not labour the point, Kissinger is shown to have remedied the deficiency exposed in *Negotiation from Strength*. That is to say, he based his policy on an acute perception of America's overall strength relative to its communist adversaries. In exchange for their easing the way for a face-saving settlement in Vietnam, he could offer the Soviet Union a relaxation of economic restrictions, and China strategic reassurance vis-à-vis the perceived Soviet threat. Detente, of course, also signified shared benefits, in particular a limitation of the strategic arms competition, but did not signify a general relaxation of the Cold War conflict, merely its pursuit at lower levels of tension. Just how robustly Kissinger could pursue American interests is shown in his manipulation of the October 1973 crisis in the Middle East to exclude the Soviet Union from its resolution and, as it proved, from a major role in subsequent Middle Eastern diplomacy.

At the time of its publication the book offered a discerning interpretation of the detente and a persuasive rebuttal of many of the polemical charges levelled against détente diplomacy. From today's vantage point, notwithstanding or perhaps because of the vast literature that has accumulated, it stands up remarkably well as an overview, and also a reminder of central issues and insights half-submerged in the subsequent accumulation of voluminous specialised studies of the period.

Similarly, although for different reasons, *The Conventions of Crisis* remains of more than historical interest. At the time it offered both an introductory overview and well-informed reflections on what was, arguably, the central problem for Cold War policy-making, vis-à-vis how best to cope with the crises that appeared to be built into the superpower relationship. Like most of the earlier literature on the topic, it can be read as a historical document: a statement of how things looked at the time. Some of its suggestions were superseded by the vast scholarly literature of the following years, much of it highly specialised and even more firmly embedded in the context of the Cold War. What stands out today, however, is that this slim volume also raises issues that were not followed up, or only to a very limited extent—for example, her image of the 'crisis slide', or the relationship between external and 'intra-mural' crises, and even the nature and significance of conventions in this context and, by implication, of their absence. Thanks to its wide-ranging, essay-like character, *The Conventions of Crisis* still has much to offer to those who might seek orientation to the problems raised by crisis diplomacy in quite changed circumstances.

How might one best locate her work in relation to the traditions of international thought, and to the contemporary discipline of international relations? Most readers would place her in the realist tradition—that of 'classical realism', drawing on the humanities, not the neorealism of contemporary American theory, based on a narrow conception of social science theorising. She prefers to characterise her approach not as realist but as traditional analysis: 'in the sense that it derives from the tradition of reflection on political and diplomatic and strategic events that goes back to Thucydides ... and uses rather simple and traditional concepts and ... vocabulary'.[3] And she refers to the formative influence of Martin Wight, for whom international relations could never be subsumed under a single theoretical approach but required an appreciation of the insights afforded by multiple perspectives. Even if we, her readers, want to insist that the message that comes through is unmistakably realist, her particular version of realism, and the richness and subtlety of her arguments, show the imprint of Wight's multi-perspectival thinking.

Classical realism, grounded in history and the humanities, is out of fashion in the contemporary international relations discipline, especially in the US, even though it remains alive and well in the policy journals. But times may be changing. Leading academic journals, even in the US, now invite contributions from 'the variety of intellectual traditions included under the rubric of international relations', to quote one formulation.[4] It cannot be said that classical realism, or even 'traditional analysis', has been finally superseded.

Even more unfashionable, however, is her Wight-like scepticism concerning theory and her total disdain for methodology.[5] Arguably, the discipline's current

---

3   Coral Bell, 'Journey with Alternative Maps', in J Kruzel and JN Rosenau, (eds), *Journeys through World Politics: Autobiographical Reflections of Thirty-four Academic Travelers*, Lexington Books, Lexington, 1989, p. 344.
4   The policy statement of *International Studies Quarterly*, each issue.
5   For her own comments on her 'marked resistance to the use of the word 'theory'', see Bell, 'Journey with Alternative Maps', pp. 347-8). For Wight's scepticism, see Martin Wight, 'Why is there no International Theory?', in Herbert Butterfield and Martin Wight (eds), *Diplomatic Investigations: Essays in the Theory of International Politics*, George Allen & Unwin, London, 1966, pp. 17–34.

preoccupation with methodology is excessive and a robust affirmation of the use of everyday language in academic writing is a useful corrective. However, it has come to be accepted in international relations, as in the other social sciences, that even when explicit theory is absent, research and scholarship are guided by theoretical assumptions. Of course, there is much bad theorising, but the answer cannot be to reject theory as such, but rather to enhance one's awareness of the strengths and weaknesses of different theories, and of one's own theoretical presuppositions.

Coral Bell's writings, like those of many historians, leave it to the reader to tease out the theoretical assumptions that underlie the analysis. It is instructive to attempt this, if only in order to locate her work more confidently within the spectrum of classical realist ideas. My reading is that it is at the opposite pole from the realism that postulates harsh necessities, inevitabilities or structural imperatives. It is a realism that highlights the scope for political and diplomatic choice, not only in the case of a superpower such as the United States but also with respect to Australia—not all the time, but much more than is generally recognised.[6] The constraints that figure most prominently in her narratives stem from domestic politics and the fixed beliefs of decision-makers and those in their milieu. If this reading is correct, her version of realism is a much-needed corrective to the systemic, structural emphases in the prevailing neorealist doctrine. But why is this not made explicit? There may be art as much as modesty in the disclaiming of theoretical intent: a theory is never so persuasive as when it is securely embedded in a good narrative.

---

6 On Australia, see for example, Coral Bell, 'Introduction', in her *Dependent Ally: A Study in Australian Foreign Policy*, 3rd edn, Allen & Unwin, Sydney 1993.

Part 3: The Practice of Power Politics

9. Realist Optimist: Coral Bell's Contribution to Australian Foreign and Defence Policy[1]

Brendan Taylor

In a collection of essays dedicated to the memory of TB Millar, Coral Bell described Millar as a scholar 'never given to provincialism: he was very much a citizen of the larger Western world, deeply fascinated by the problems of the East-West balance during the Cold War years'.[2] This description is one that perhaps applies even more aptly to Coral and her work. Her preoccupation was very much the diplomatic and strategic relations between the great powers of what Coral liked to term 'the central balance'. Yet like Millar, a significant portion of her career was also spent advancing the study of Australian foreign and defence policy. As this chapter goes on to demonstrate, much of her work in this area addressed the interplay between the central balance and Australian policy. It did so by bringing a formidable grasp of history together with an enduring desire to decipher the contours of the emerging international political landscape. And despite her realist proclivities, Coral was also—by her own admission—very much the optimist regarding Australia's prospects in that emerging landscape.

The Past as Prologue

Coral's earliest experiences of Australian foreign and defence policy revolved much more around its practical elements than the academic study thereof. In a number of respects, she experienced the use of force against Australia in the most direct, even personal of ways. She spent three years (1942–1945) during the Second World War, for instance, in a University of Sydney physics laboratory which assisted with the degaussing of ships. In a short memoir of her career, she recalls purchasing a rather large poker for protection against any Japanese invasion. In characteristically colourful terms, she writes of her intent 'to sell my life or virtue as dearly as possible when they came up the garden path.'

1   A version of the essay has previously been published by Taylor & Francis Ltd., as: Brendan Taylor, 'Coral Bell's contribution to Australian foreign policy', *Australian Journal of International Affairs*, vol. 59, no. 3, 2005, pp. 257–260; and has been reprinted by permission of the publisher.
2   Coral Bell, 'Preface', in Coral Bell, ed., *Nation, Region and Context: Studies in Peace and War in Honour of Professor T.B. Millar*, Canberra Papers on Strategy and Defence no. 112, 1995, Strategic and Defence Studies Centre, Canberra, 1995, p. xiii.

Unduly dramatic as that may now seem in light of evidence that the threat of Japanese invasion was perhaps more imagined than real,[3] Coral elsewhere does recall hearing 'a Japanese shell or two whistl[ing] overhead during the submarine raid of 1942.'[4] More tragically, she also lost her 'first love' during the Papua New Guinea campaign.

As the Second World War drew to a close, Coral decided to contribute to the practice of Australian foreign policy by entering the diplomatic service. She moved to Canberra in 1945 as one of ten new recruits—Coral being the only female among them. 'Doc' Evatt was the Minister for External Affairs at that time and Coral's new career brought her into contact with a number of historical figures of Australian foreign and defence policy, including the formidable Sir Arthur Tange.[5]

Her first assignment was under John Burton in the Department's United Nations Division. She moved subsequently to work on Southeast Asia, becoming the only desk officer in a small department—even by today's standards—to work on this entire sub-region. Coral was later dispatched to Wellington, New Zealand—a posting she regarded as a 'wooden spoon'. But it was a posting which saw her involved as a 'bit player' in negotiations leading up to the signing of the ANZUS (Australia New Zealand United States) agreement. Again in her memoir, Coral recounts a secret visit by then Head of the Department, Alan Watt, to talk the New Zealanders out of siding with Britain. When Watt arrived, the High Commissioner and Official Secretary were elsewhere, leaving Coral as the only staffer 'holding the fort.'

Notwithstanding her involvement in the practice of Australian foreign policy during such a formative period, Coral never made any secret of the fact that she disliked diplomatic life and felt immeasurably more comfortable in the corridors of academia. She was never attracted to the prospect of being a mere 'cog in the wheel' of government. At a more personal level, the more debauched side of diplomatic life was anathema to Coral's character. As she recalls:

> [T]he diplomatic life-style did not really suit me. I have never been, in any of its senses, a party girl, and diplomacy is a very party-ridden occupation, especially in a small post, as Wellington then was. If you meet roughly the same fifty or so people at cocktail and dinner parties five evenings a week, you tend to run out of small talk, which has never been my favourite form of conversation anyway. I needed a more reflective kind of life.

3 For further reading see Peter Dean, ed., *Australia 1942: In the Shadow of War*, Cambridge University Press, Port Melbourne, 2013.
4 Coral Bell, 'Australians and Strategic Inquiry', in Bell, *Nation, Region and Context*, p. 51.
5 For further reading see Peter Edwards, *Arthur Tange: Last of the Mandarins*, Allen & Unwin, Sydney, 2006.

Living with Giants

After six years in the diplomatic service, Coral left Australia and spent most of the next two and a half decades in the United Kingdom, where she first went to take up graduate study at the London School of Economics (LSE). Here she encountered the renowned International Relations theorist Martin Wight— who Coral identified as 'the chief intellectual influence of my entire life' and frequently described in conversation as her 'guru.' During this period she also worked as a research officer at the Royal Institute of International Affairs (Chatham House), where the renowned historian Arnold J Toynbee handed her the editorial reins to *Survey of International Affairs*—a flagship Chatham House publication and almost certainly the most authoritative textbook in international politics at that time.

Coral went on to take up an appointment at the University of Manchester. In 1959 she also held a Rockefeller Fellowship in the US, which allowed her to spend time as a visiting academic at Columbia University and the School of Advanced International Studies in Washington. Over the course of this entire period, Coral came into contact with key figures in the fields of strategic studies and international relations, including the likes of Alastair Buchan, Hedley Bull, Michael Howard and Henry Kissinger.

These encounters were significant from an Australian perspective in that they raised the intellectual profile of analysis from this country. Denis Healey, the former British Labor MP and one of the founding fathers of the International Institute for Strategic Studies (IISS), observed in his own memoir that 'from the middle fifties Australia has contributed far more to international understanding of defence problems than any country of similar size.'[6] Certainly he had Coral in mind when making this observation. Secretary of the Department of Foreign Affairs, Sir Keith Waller, made a similar observation of Coral in the early 1970s when he wrote that 'her work has brought a new lustre to the reputation of Australia in all countries where people follow the serious study of foreign affairs.'[7]

Coral herself was never shy about referring to her antipodean origins and offering a distinctly Australian perspective on international politics. In her classic 1968 *Adelphi* paper on the Asian balance of power, for instance, she stated from the outset that:

---

6   Denis Healey, *The Time of My Life*, Michael Joseph, London, 1989, p. 192.
7   Cited in Coral Bell, *Crises and Australian Diplomacy*, Arthur F Yencken Memorial Lecture 1972, Australian National University Press, 1973, p. 1.

It will be an Australian view in the sense that the author, as an Australian, must be conscious that her own country's efforts to provide for its future security should include some assessment of the prospects for such a balance. Perhaps there is a certain appropriateness to an Australian examination of this question, since Australians are the only group of Westerners who must remain fully and inescapably vulnerable to the diplomatic stresses arising in Asia, on whose periphery they live or die.[8]

By the 1960s, however, Coral was beginning to feel the pull of home, a feeling exacerbated by the unexpected passing of her father (Coral's mother had also passed away unexpectedly, of a brain aneurism, when Coral was a child). She thus returned to Australia for four years during the early 1960s as the University of Sydney's first appointment in the field of international relations. Here she first encountered a young Desmond Ball, another emerging Australian scholar of strategic studies who, like Coral, would go on to make a significant impact internationally.[9]

Yet for a scholar really beginning to make her mark on the international scene, one gets the sense that Australia was simply too small and too remote for Coral at that time. In her memoir she recalls that 'Australia seemed suddenly to be in a lonely place, internationally, diplomatically and strategically'. To be sure, amongst her students at Sydney there were some who would make their own mark internationally, such as Richard Butler and Martin Indyk. Owen Harries, who would go on to become editor of the prominent American policy journal, *The National Interest*, was also a colleague and 'cherished friend.' Yet Coral 'did not find the intellectual climate of Australia in the late Menzies period much to my liking.' Hence, when the offer of a Readership at LSE came along, Coral 'was not much tempted to resist it'.

Coral retained some interest in Australian foreign and defence policy during her time away. In 1972, for instance, she delivered the Arthur F Yencken Memorial Lecture on the theme of 'Crises and Australian Diplomacy.' She divided the lecture into two parts, delivered over two evenings. The first addressed the nature of crises more generally and how they are managed by the great powers. The second examined their impact upon Australia and what, if anything, Australian diplomacy might do to ameliorate or influence them.[10]

When Coral returned permanently to Australia in the late 1970s—to take up a position as Senior Research Fellow in the Department of International Relations

---

8   Coral Bell, *The Asian Balance of Power: A Comparison with European Precedents*, Adelphi Paper no. 44, International Institute for Strategic Studies, London, February 1968, p. 1.
9   For further reading on the life and work of Ball see Brendan Taylor, Nicholas Farrelly and Sheryn Lee (eds), *Insurgent Intellectual: Essays in Honour of Professor Desmond Ball*, Institute of Southeast Asian Studies, Singapore, 2012.
10   Coral Bell, *Crises and Australian Diplomacy*.

at The Australian National University (ANU)—this interplay between the global and Australian policy remained a theme of her research. For instance, in 1980 she edited a volume considering choices in Australian foreign and defence policy, including a chapter which Coral contributed entitled 'The Central Balance and Australian Policy.' As she wrote in that chapter, 'Australia's security has always, one may argue, been taken by its decision-makers to depend on its status as a protégé of one of the central-balance powers'.[11]

This latter observation was a central element of what is almost certainly Coral's most significant contribution to the study of Australian foreign and defence policy. *Dependent Ally* was first published in 1984 and went on to appear in at least three different editions. It examined the evolution of Australia's relations with Britain and the United States over the previous two hundred years. It did so with an eye to illustrating some of the dilemmas of diplomatic and strategic dependency, as well as some of the costs and benefits of alliance.

One of the most enduring conclusions to emerge from Coral's sweeping study was the manner in which Australia's dependency on its great and powerful friends has not remained entirely consistent but has instead been subject to a variety of influences. Foremost amongst these, *Dependent Ally* concluded, was the personality and assumptions of Australia's chief decision-maker at any given time. As Coral so colourfully put it:

> One might see the history as that of a succession of chefs with the same basic raw material to work on, and much the same 'notional preferences' among the consumers. The flavour and texture and palatability of what is achieved will vary chiefly in accordance with their respective skills and techniques, because there are not many other factors of variation.[12]

A standout feature of *Dependent Ally* is Coral's deep knowledge and application of history which is, indeed, a feature of much of her work. In surveying the history of the British–Australian relationship, for instance, she reaches back to the 1850s to an episode during the Crimean War which she argues highlights some of the central problems of the relationship which would culminate with Australia's 'turn to America' almost a century later.[13] Later in the book she again draws comparisons between the time at which she was writing and the world a hundred years previous: 'the diplomatic wheel seems to have turned full circle

---

11 'The Central Balance and Australian Policy', in Coral Bell (ed), *Agenda for the Eighties*, Australian National University Press, Canberra, 1980, p. 6. A decade on, Coral edited a second such volume which included a similarly titled contribution. See Coral Bell, 'The Changing Central Balance and Australian Policy', in Coral Bell (ed), *Agenda for the Nineties: Australian Choices in Foreign and Defence Policy*, Longman Cheshire, Melbourne, 1991, pp. 1–23.

12 Coral Bell, *Dependent Ally: A Study in Australian Foreign Policy*, Allen & Unwin, Sydney, 1984, p. 175.

13 ibid., p. 7.

over a century, Russia being a Pacific power in the 1990s as it had been in the 1890s. Then it was a putative adversary, to be succeeded by quite an assortment of other actual or putative adversaries'.[14]

Like so many scholars of international relations and strategic studies, Coral spent the early years of the 1990s adjusting to and trying to make sense of the collapse of the Soviet Union and the ending of the Cold War. In 1991 for instance, she produced a short monograph examining Australia's alliance options in a world transformed. The potential significance of these shifts was captured by Coral's observation that they represented 'nothing less than the disappearance of the whole organizing principle of the world in which ANZUS was created'.[15] Notwithstanding these epochal changes, Coral remained convinced that Australia's alliance with the United States would endure over the short to medium term. This was in large part due to her pessimism that a still nascent Asian regionalism could deliver a satisfactory alternative. Over the longer term, she presciently observed, the 'central balance' was likely to evolve in ways not necessarily as conducive to Australia as had been the case previously. Against that backdrop, Coral posited that the expectation of strong backing from its American ally—particularly during a crisis—would remain critically importantly to Canberra.[16]

Next only to *Dependent Ally*, however, Coral's most substantial contribution in the field of Australian foreign policy came in the form of her 2005 Australian Strategic Policy Institute (ASPI) paper *Living with Giants*.[17] In this study, Coral peered several decades into the future in an attempt to decipher the shape of the emerging landscape of international politics. Her focus was primarily upon the security implications of population growth and, in the main, the fact that the world several decades from now will be comprised of at least nineteen societies of at least a hundred million people. Of particular significance to Australia, ten of these would be located within Australia's own area of primary strategic concern.

Despite the potential for a re-run of the 1930s conflict between the 'haves' and the 'have nots'—albeit on a much larger scale—Coral saw at least two positive diplomatic patterns emerging as part of this new landscape. The first was the beginnings of a 'regional security community' built around the fledging ASEAN-plus-three countries, as well as Australia and New Zealand. Second, she also suggested that the US-led unipolar world was fast reaching its twilight and

---

14   ibid., p. 185.
15   Coral Bell, *Australia's Alliance Options: Prospect and Retrospect in a World of Change*, Australian Foreign Policy Publications Program, The Australian National University, Canberra, 1991, p. 2.
16   ibid, p. 57.
17   Coral Bell, *Living with Giants: Finding Australia's place in a more complex world*, Strategy Report, Australian Strategic Policy Institute, Canberra, April 2005.

that it could be replaced by a global 'concert of powers'—a concept discussed at greater length by Hugh White in his contribution to this volume—comprising at least eight nuclear powers and possibly other countries. Coral saw such a structure as a far safer alternative than a competitive 'balance of power' between these 'giants.'

Coral's exploration of the emerging landscape of international politics and its relevance to Australia continued in her 2007 paper *The End of the Vasco da Gama Era*, which was published under the auspices of the Lowy Institute for International Policy.[18] In this study, Coral identified four powerful historical factors that were shaping this landscape. First, the end of the Vasco da Gama era—a term she used to refer to the end of the five hundred years of Western ascendency over Asia. Second, she again pointed to the end of the 'unipolar moment.' Third, a changing distribution of power both between and within states. And finally, environmental change.

Of these four forces, Coral saw the end of the Vasco da Gama era and environmental change as having the most significant ramifications for Australia. But she was also optimistic regarding the prospects for order in the emerging multipolar structure, namely because the greatest challenges to that order—the 'Jihadists', climate change and the proliferation of nuclear weapons to small powers—were all emerging outside the circle of the six most obvious great powers of the new order—the US, the European Union (EU), China, India, Russia and Japan. This, Coral argued, was likely to facilitate cooperation amongst the six with respect to these challenges.

Throughout her long and distinguished career, optimism remained a consistent feature of Coral's work. And it certainly rings through strongly in the conclusion to *The End of the Vasco da Gama Era*:

> But there is no reason for Canberra to view with apprehension the coming of a prospective multipolar world balance. We have no special enemy among the six great powers who appear likely to share the governance of that emerging world. ... As middle powers go, Australia is exceptionally well endowed with both economic and strategic assets. ... The United States will remain the paramount power in the society of states, only in a multipolar world instead of a unipolar or bipolar one.[19]

Yet this sense of optimism should not be mistaken for complacency. Rather, *Living with Giants* and *The End of the Vasco da Gama Era* both illustrate the extent to which Coral was consistently pushing the envelope in an unrelenting

---

18   Coral Bell, *The End of the Vasco da Gama Era: The Next Landscape of World Politics*, Lowy Institute Paper 21, Lowy Institute for International Policy, Sydney, 2007.

19   ibid, pp. 52–53.

drive to look imaginatively toward the future. This is certainly made clear in the conclusion to *Living with Giants*, which contains echoes of Barbara Tuchman's influential history of the opening days of the First World War, *The Guns of August*, and its central argument that miscalculation and a failure of imagination sent the European powers tumbling into the abyss of war.[20] In Coral's terms:

> This essay was inspired by the conclusion of the September 11 Commission report, naming a 'failure of imagination' as the origin of the disaster. Its speculations have been intended to promote the avoidance of a similar danger for Australia.[21]

Influencing the Climate of Opinion

Coral's contributions to Australian foreign and defence policy clearly extends beyond the scholarly works referred to in this chapter. To be sure, her impact has not been as direct as some of her long-standing academic colleagues, such as Paul Dibb whose 1986 *Review of Australia's Defence Capabilities* has had such a profound influence on the shape of Australian strategic policy during the period since,[22] or Desmond Ball, whose path-breaking work on US strategic installations in Australia markedly expanded the contours of the public debate on this subject.[23]

It could be argued, however, that Coral was more a believer in the power of analysis to filter its way indirectly into the system. As she once observed, 'it is of course always difficult to show direct causal connection between the choices of decision-makers and the analyses published by outsiders, but such analyses do help create the climate of opinion within which both the policy makers and the decision makers live, work, and have their being.'[24]

During her career, Coral influenced that climate of opinion in a number of ways. Internationally, she did so (and lifted Australia's diplomatic profile in the process) through her conversations with prominent statesmen—such as Henry Kissinger, who has cited her prominently in his own work[25] —and through her appearance in a number of high-profile American policy journals, such as *Foreign Affairs*, *The National Interest*, and *The American Interest*.[26]

---

20 Barbara Tuchman, *The Guns of August*, MacMillan, New York, 1962.
21 Bell, *Living with Giants*, p. 55.
22 Report to the Minister for Defence by Mr Paul Dibb, *Review of Australia's Defence Capabilities*, Australian Government Printing Service, Canberra, 1986.
23 See, for example, Desmond Ball, *A Suitable Piece of Real Estate: American Installations in Australia*, Hale and Iremonger, Sydney, 1980.
24 Bell, 'Australians and Strategic Inquiry', p. 70.
25 See, for example, Henry Kissinger, *Does America Need a Foreign Policy?*, 2nd edn, Touchstone, New York, 2002, p. 288.
26 See, for example, Coral Bell, 'The Twilight of the Unipolar World', *The American Interest*, vol. 1, no. 2, Winter 2005, pp. 18–29.

Coral also influenced that climate of opinion through the people she worked with, taught and mentored. Former students recall with fondness the seminars and now almost legendary morning teas which were held during the 1970s and 1980s at the ANU HC Coombs building. Through her presence and participation in these, Coral contributed in a substantial way to the education of a significant number of emerging scholars. Many of those subsequently moved on to take up senior positions in academia, government and the military.

Moreover, during a period when women were woefully under-represented in the Australian foreign and defence policy debate, it is worth keeping in mind that Coral served for over half a century—ever since her appointment as one of Australia's first female diplomats—as a mentor and role model for female scholars and practitioners working in these fields. In March 2005 for instance, she was the keynote speaker at the inaugural meeting of the Canberra chapter of the 'Women in International Security' initiative.

From the Shadows

Despite her passing, Coral's work continues to exhibit particular relevance to a number of Australia's contemporary foreign and security policy debates. There has been recent speculation, for instance, that Washington is becoming increasingly frustrated by Canberra's unwillingness to assume a greater share of the defence burden at a time when the US is hurting financially. These tensions were apparent in the lead up to the 2012 AUSMIN talks, for instance, when Pacific Commander Admiral Samuel Locklear and Assistant Secretary of State Kurt Campbell each expressed concerns about the Australian defence budget.[27] Speaking with an *Australian Financial Review* journalist in August 2013, former Deputy Secretary of State Richard Armitage was even more direct, arguing that Australia simply cannot continue 'free-riding' on its alliance with America.[28]

While these are indeed valid criticisms that should not be taken lightly, Coral's work reminds us that they are not particularly new ones. In *Dependent Ally*, for instance, she makes the following observation regarding the pattern of commitment of Australian forces in support of allied operations and the levels of funding budgeted for defence:

> The forces sent were as near to 'token' size as the ally concerned could
> be induced to acquiesce in. Australian defence policy-makers seem to

---

27   See Peter Jennings, 'Trunk Call for AUSMIN', *The Strategist*, Australian Strategic Policy Institute, 12 November 2012.
28   Christopher Joye, 'Free Ride on US Defence Must Stop', *Australian Financial Review*, 19 August 2013.

have been as passive, politically, as any liberal could wish, not activist or adroit, even about getting what they would regard as funds adequate to the sort of armoury Australia needed.[29]

Coral's work is also of continuing relevance to what is arguably Australia's leading foreign and defence policy debate of recent years regarding this country's response to the rise of China. A central figure in this debate, Hugh White, has written extensively on the dilemmas he believes Australia faces given that its leading economic and strategic partners—China and the US—are on opposite sides of a deepening strategic competition. He sees the possibility looming—potentially sooner than many analysts may believe—of Canberra having to choose between the US and China in the context, for instance, of an armed clash between China and Japan over the disputed Senkaku/Diaoyu Islands.[30] However, by observing that there has traditionally been a 'slow motion quality' to Australia's responses to changed strategic circumstances, Coral reminds us that White's 'China choice' is quite unlikely to play out in the manner he describes, if indeed there is even a choice of that nature to be made at this present juncture in history.[31]

Indeed, rather than a stark choice occasioned by deepening strategic rivalry between the US and China, the next two to three decades is much more likely to involve a mix of cooperation and competition between these two heavyweights. Contemporary analytical frameworks for understanding the US–China relationship have thus far proven unable to anticipate and to accommodate these dynamics particularly well. Instead, they have tended to gravitate towards one of two opposing poles. At one end of the spectrum, pessimists such as John Mearsheimer and Aaron Friedberg point to the inevitability of strategic competition between the US and China.[32] At the other, optimists such as Henry Kissinger, Zbigniew Brzezinski and White himself have instead pointed to the possibility of a power-sharing agreement between Beijing and Washington. This idea reached the peak of its popularity during the 2008–2009 global financial crisis in the form of calls for a 'G2'.[33]

Developed during the 1960s, Coral's concept of a 'shadow condominium' offers a 'third way' between these two diametrically opposing positions and one that is potentially better able to capture to competitive and cooperative dynamics of

---

29   Bell, *Dependent Ally*, p. 176.

30   See, for example, Hugh White, 'Australia's Choice: Will the Land Down Under Pick the United States or China?', *Foreign Affairs*, 4 September 2013.

31   See Bell, *Dependent Ally*, p. 178.

32   See, for example, John J Mearsheimer, *The Tragedy of Great Power Politics*, WW Norton & Company, New York, 2001; and Aaron L. Friedberg, *A Contest for Supremacy: China, America, and the Struggle for Mastery in Asia*, W.W. Norton and Company, New York, 2011.

33   See, for example, Zbigniew Brzezinski, 'The Group of Two That Could Change the World', *Financial Times*, 14 July 2009.

the emerging US–China relationship.[34] Inspired by the dynamics of superpower diplomacy during the Cuban Missile Crisis (which marked its fiftieth anniversary in the same year as Coral's passing), the 'shadow condominium' that she referred to was a temporary power-sharing arrangement that emerged during periods of acute crisis engaging the interests of the two dominant powers. But once the danger had passed, this arrangement retreated 'into the shadows of the future' and default adversarial postures resumed.

Ever the optimist—albeit one with strong realist proclivities—Coral maintained that there was always a prospect for the condominium to re-emerge out of those shadows during times of deep crisis. In her view, periods of power transition are especially conducive to such arrangements because they are invariably dangerous and difficult. The primary function of the 'shadow condominium' during such periods is to provide stability through joint great power management of the balance of power.

In the context of Asia's current power shift, the best evidence that Bell's 1960s template applies aptly to US–China relations comes from the Korean Peninsula. To be sure, strategic competition between China and the US has been a perennial feature of security politics surrounding this flashpoint.[35] Arguably of greater interest, however, has been the cooperation that has occurred between Beijing and Washington during periods of crisis.

In early 2003, following the collapse of the 1994 Agreed Framework, for instance, Beijing and Washington worked to initiate three party talks with North Korea which subsequently morphed into a larger and moderately successful Six Party format. Again in 2006, in the midst of heightened tensions following North Korea's first nuclear test, American and Chinese officials came together to bring North Korea back to the negotiating table.[36] In 2010, following the North's November bombardment of Yeonpyeong Island, tensions heightened to the point where highly respected analysts such as Victor Cha pointed to the possibility of all out conflict between the two Koreas.[37] By December, however, Beijing and Washington were again reportedly working together to create calm.[38]

This pattern recurred once more following the sudden death of North Korean leader Kim Jong-Il in late 2011. The US and China maintained very close contact

---

34 Coral's concept of a 'shadow condominium' is outlined in Coral Bell, *The Debatable Alliance: An Essay in Anglo-American Relations*, Chatham House Essays No.3, Oxford University Press, London, 1964, pp. 108–113.
35 See Benjamin Schreer and Brendan Taylor, 'The Korean Crises and Sino-American Rivalry', *Survival*, vol. 53, no. 1, February-March 2011, pp. 13–19.
36 For a useful summary of US–China cooperation during this period see Bonnie S Glaser and Wang Liang, 'North Korea: The Beginning of a China–US Partnership', *The Washington Quarterly*, vol. 31, no. 1, Summer 2008, pp. 165–180.
37 Victor Cha, 'What to do about N. Korean Aggression?', *The Chosun Ilbo (English edition)*, 6 December 2010.
38 See Mark Landler, 'China's North Korea Shift Helps US Relations', *New York Times*, 23 December 2010.

in the aftermath of that event. Indeed, during a visit to Beijing at the time, Assistant Secretary of State Kurt Campbell spoke in terms not inconsistent with Coral's 'shadow condominium' concept when intimating that 'I think the US and China share a strong determination to maintain peace and stability'.[39]

Will a US–China 'shadow condominium' manifest itself in the case of future strategic crises—in the South China Sea, the East China Sea, or over Taiwan—if and when these emerge? Only time will tell. Yet aside from the fact that it was conceived by one of our great strategic intellectuals, Australian foreign and defence policy-makers might do well in the meantime to entertain and further explore the possibility.

First, it offers a more realistic way of thinking about US-China relations than a more formal, institutionalised power-sharing arrangement, such as the 'G2'. Beijing and Washington simply do not share the same common values or compatible strategic cultures necessary to sustain an arrangement of that nature.[40] Second, a US–China 'shadow condominium' will be more palatable to countries— including Japan and India—who fear their potential marginalisation under a more formal US–China power-sharing arrangement because they read it as a step towards some mild form of world government. Finally, and most importantly, a US–China 'shadow condominium' is also a more attractive proposition than the intense and inherently unstable US–China strategic competition that some analysts predict, along with the stark strategic choices that such competition would likely imply for Australia.

---

39   US Department of State, Kurt M. Campbell, Assistant Secretary, Bureau of East Asian and Pacific Affairs, 'Remarks to the Media on Departure at the Beijing Capital Airport', 4 January 2012.

40   For a useful critique of the 'G2' concept see Elizabeth C Economy and Adam Segal, 'The G2 Mirage: Why the United States and China are Not Ready to Upgrade Ties', *Foreign Affairs*, vol. 88, no. 3, May/June 2009, pp.14–23.

10. Interpreting the Cold War

Michael Wesley

Coral Bell watched the Cold War take shape from one of ten offices in a building known as West Block, where Australia's Department of External Affairs was accommodated during the 1940s and early 1950s. There is an old saying that even the greatest diplomats never lose the desk officer's eye and fascination for the telling detail that hints at the big strategic picture; in all of Coral's writings on the Cold War one can feel her attentive mind pouring over papers, opinion and quotes, the strategist-as-detective amassing the fine detail and the telling *bon mots* into a masterful narrative. That Coral's first professional engagement with international affairs was as a practitioner had a lasting impact on her work; that this particular practitioner began watching the world as the reality of the Cold War became very real to Australia was to structure how she interpreted that conflict from beginning to end.

In her many writings on the Cold War, Coral always showed the practitioner's sensitivity to the often galling realities of policy-making. For example, she instinctively sensed George Kennan's frustration that, despite being in charge of Policy Planning in the State Department, he was prevented by security barriers from knowing America's actual military strength, and thus was unable to make a clear judgement about the relationship between America's commitments and capabilities.[1] Coral's practitioner's view of the unfolding of the Cold War also contributed to her distinctly Anglo-centric view of the conflict. A striking thread of continuity through all of her writings on the Cold War is her determination to make the point that the free world was not led by America alone, but by an Anglo–American condominium. As David Lowe and Christopher Waters chronicle, the early years of the Cold War saw a resurgence of Anglophilia in Australia, which the Pacific War and the American alliance had eroded during the 1940s.[2] Between 1948 and 1952, Australia's strategic preoccupations changed from regional worries about Japan's resurgence to global concerns about the Cold War—and to supporting the Anglo-American cause in the global struggle with communism. Coral was at pains to point out at several junctures that the eventually successful western strategy in the Cold War, from the Marshall Plan to the 'scaffolding' that became NATO to the integration of West Germany into the western alliance was as much London's as Washington's design. Indeed,

---

1   Coral Bell, *Negotiation from Strength: A Study in the Politics of Power*, Chatto & Windus, London, 1962, p. 36.
2   David Lowe, *Menzies and the 'Great World Struggle': Australia's Cold War, 1948–1954*, UNSW Press, Sydney, 1999; Christopher Waters, *The Empire Fracture: Anglo-Australian Conflict in the 1940s*, Australian Scholarly Publishing, Melbourne, 1995.

there is more than a hint of Harold Macmillan's belief that Britain could play the tempering role of the 'Greek' nuance and intellectualism in strategy to the Americans' 'Roman' muscle when she observed that the design for NATO was actually 'a return to the long-standing British tradition of a continental alliance as the basis of a balance of power coalition against any new potential contender for European hegemony'.[3]

But none of this is to argue that Coral Bell was either a detail-mired pedant or a slavish Anglo-booster. What really emerges from her writings on the Cold War is the mind and judgements of a master strategist. Without being cased in the ponderous methodology or self-congratulatory philosophics of American and British international relations, the theoretical and conceptual gems that pepper her Cold War writings nestle amidst her elegant prose, guaranteed to cause the reader to pause and look into the middle distance regularly. Her wonderful use of level-of-analysis reasoning (without ever referring to that awful phrase) to distinguish between containment and negotiation-from-strength is one example.[4] Her incisive contribution to alliance theory, in terms of a balance between 'net producers' and 'net consumers' of security, is another.[5]

Coral was also a thinker who had the uncanny knack of previewing debates and controversies decades before others were to use them to make their names. Her discussion of mutually-abrasive values systems arising from the empowerment of newly-independent states, particularly in the wake of the Khomeinist revolution in Iran, prefigured Bull's and Watson's writings and Huntington's 'clash of civilizations' by years.[6] Similarly her considerations of the rise and origins of America's neoconservatives, and their philosophical and policy differences from realists and liberals, preceded the arrival of the George W Bush administration by well over a decade.[7] In retrospect, Coral's clear and balanced discussion of the neo-cons, with its subtle undercurrent of irony, stands as still the best there is, even after the avalanche of analyses that accompanied the Bush years.

The Cold War was the conflict that animated Coral Bell's writings. She pushed and probed at the confrontation, teasing out the inner logics of its grand strategies and concepts and subjecting them to the judgement of her incisive mind. Even when she confined herself to writing about Australia, she began and ended her

---

3   Coral Bell, *The Cold War in Retrospect: Diplomacy, Strategy and Regional Impact'*, Working Paper no. 298, Strategic and Defence Studies Centre, The Australian National University, Canberra. 1996, p. 3.
4   Bell, *Negotiation From Strength*, p. 30.
5   ibid., pp. 172–173.
6   Coral Bell, *President Carter and Foreign Policy: The Costs of Virtue?*, Canberra Studies in World Affairs, The Australian National University, no. 1, 1980, pp. 100–101
7   Coral Bell, *The Reagan Paradox: American Foreign Policy in the 1980s*, Edward Elgar, Aldershot, 1989, pp. 5–12.

analysis with the 'central balance'.[8] She never tried to set herself the task of writing a grand all-encompassing account of the Cold War, probably precisely because the practitioner in her knew such a task would see the telling detail be overwhelmed by the straitjacket of narrative; the scholar in her probably also knew that the analytical meat lay in isolating and investigating aspects of the bigger conflict. To my reading, Coral Bell interpreted the Cold War according to six broad preoccupations. Some of these preoccupations animate a single book or article. Others run through the long period of her scholarship, and with each return, a different aspect of the preoccupation is explored. Each on its own stands as a major contribution to Cold War scholarship; together they constitute a remarkable monument to understanding the defining stand-off of the twentieth century.

Democratic Alliances Versus Authoritarian Blocs

The earliest preoccupation in Coral Bell's Cold War writing is with whether democracies in an alliance are able to muster the will, strength and flexibility to prevail in a contest with an authoritarian bloc. *Negotiation From Strength* can be read as an extended analysis of the disadvantages of democratic decision-making and alliance management and strategising in an extended low-intensity confrontation such as the Cold War. Her ultimate conclusion is that, during the first decade of the Cold War, an alliance of democracies was unable to summon either the strength or to choose the right time to negotiate based on a judgement of the most favourable correlation of forces. While her apprehensions about the authoritarian advantage in strength and negotiation were inevitably to wane with the passing of the years, Coral's sober pessimism about democratic strategising and alliance politics remained undimmed.

From the start, Coral regarded military alliances as a necessary weakness for the United States. While Washington needed a strategic foothold and eventual arsenal in western Europe, it bought these at the cost of difficult and at times all-consuming alliance relations. 'There are', she wrote,

> two surprising things about the history of NATO. The first is that its strategic concepts have borne so little relation to the ostensible political or diplomatic ambitions of its members. The second is that though the states to whom was allotted the task of raising the forces proposed for the Central Front have included some of the most notable and successful

---

8   Coral Bell, 'The Central Balance and Australian Policy' in Coral Bell (ed) *Agenda for the Eighties: Contexts of Australian Choices in Foreign and Defence Policy,* Australian National University Press, Canberra, 1980.

military powers in modern history … they have never succeeded in reaching actual force figures commensurate with even their minimal strategic objectives, … a politically dismaying demonstration of their inability to match intention and performance unless the knife is at their throats.[9]

For Coral, the problem had two parts: democracy and alliances. Each seemed to exacerbate the inability of the other to function effectively. Alliances seemed to mire strategy in a form of collective small-mindedness: 'in the nature of things, the ability of an alliance to pursue a common policy is limited and conditional: limited and conditioned by the behavior of the putative enemy, the lowest common denominator of individual cost and the highest common denominator of individual interest'.[10] Democracy on the other hand was the constant enemy of the strategist, be he Acheson, Dulles, Kissinger or Bzrezinski. Populism was heightened by the constant tension of the Cold War, forcing American policy-makers towards decisions that brought strategic disadvantage. Democracy foregrounded morale and mood as the key ingredient of Cold War policy-making: on reading Coral's account of the psychological impact on America of the triple shocks of 1949—the communist victory in China, the Soviet nuclear test, and the discovery of communist spies in the American government—one is left in little doubt about the constraints under which the Truman administration was acting.[11]

It was perhaps the difference in unity and resolve between the Cold War and the Second World War that was most dismaying. Coral was pessimistic about the 'political limitations on the ability of a government in a democracy to pursue an unpopular course of action in a period of less than immediate crisis'.[12] The problem was that in conditions of crisis, 'decisions had to be taken at great speed, with little leisure for reflection on the limits they might later impose on the negotiating position of the West'.[13] In the final analysis, the West's ability to build requisite strength in the Cold War's first decade was the result of failures in leadership, the nature of democratic institutions, and the commitment to pluralistic decision-making within countries and across the alliance.[14] On the other hand, the time at which it was most advantageous to negotiate with the Soviet Union from a position of comparative strength, Dulles was unable to do so because of the hyper-aroused state of the domestic political climate.

---

9   Bell, *Negotiation from Strength*, p. 46.
10 ibid., pp. 202–203.
11 ibid., pp. 76–77.
12 ibid., p. 47.
13 ibid., p. 47.
14 ibid., p. 191.

Coral seemed to shift in her thinking over time about whether grand strategic coups were within the capacity of democracies. At the end of *Negotiation From Strength* she concludes that democratic strategising must be from necessity about pragmatism, the finding of least-worst outcomes, a 'sophisticated Micawberism'.[15] A couple of decades later, she was not so sure. Kissinger's grand strategising as the animation of the policy of détente emerges as a case where a democracy considerably outpaces sophisticated Micawberism.[16] Carter's 'sho 'nuff' earnest idealism emerges as a more unfortunate example,[17] while Reagan's calculated bravura is judged more favourably.[18]

A Study in Competitive Psychology

Coral Bell's intuitive power is best and repeatedly illustrated by her focus on issues and tendencies that at the time were not widely known or discussed, but which later became defining frameworks of analysis. One such remarkable example occurs late in *Negotiation From Strength*, in which her discussion of the competitive psychology of Cold War strategy clearly anticipates by nearly two decades Daniel Kahneman and Amos Tversky's defining work on prospect theory and decision bias. While Kahneman and Tversky's theories were based on painstaking empirical research, Coral comes to very similar conclusions based on sheer deductive intuition.

She begins with a careful discussion of the clear conceptual differences between status quo and revisionist strategies in the Cold War. Unlike Kissinger and others who were inclined to label entire foreign policies status quo or revisionist, Coral pointed out that there were elements of status quo-ism and revisionism in both American and Soviet policy. 'There is a stronger unconscious element of revisionism in American foreign policy attitudes than Americans are usually prepared to perceive', she wrote. That revisionism was the constant desire to make the world more compatible with American principles and interests. Soviet revisionism came from the same motivation. Negotiation from strength, in these terms, meant 'an effort to improve the balance of military power, and to use your new position to seek a new status quo of a more satisfactory sort'.[19] But the revisionist policy of each threatened the status quo perceptions of the other; thus 'issues like Berlin are obviously not only important in themselves but important as psychological rallying points. The status quo is physically expressed in a number of territorial arrangements, and the demand to change

---

15   ibid., p. 189.
16   Coral Bell, *The Diplomacy of Détente: The Kissinger Era*, St Martin's Press, New York, 1977.
17   Bell, *President Carter and Foreign Policy*.
18   Bell, *The Reagan Paradox*.
19   Bell, *Negotiation from Strength*, p. 201.

one of them is heavy with psychological significance'.[20] Therefore, 'faced with the clear prospect of encroachment on its sphere of power by a dangerous enemy, a nation may stake its survival on resistance to that encroachment ... especially in a period in which the memory of Munich has been invoked unceasingly to prove that whenever anything is conceded, everything is lost'.[21]

On accepting the Nobel Prize in 2002, Kahneman said that his and Tversky's most important discovery was a pervasive decision bias they named 'loss aversion': the widespread human tendency to forego the chance of making a gain if taking that chance could also result in a loss. This had been detailed in a breakthrough article in 1979.[22] Here is Coral Bell, writing in 1962:

> The prospect of loss is a stronger motive in international affairs, as in individual ones, than the hope of gain. This may not be logical, but it is reasonable enough. The powerful forces of anger and immediate fear reinforce calculation when loss is in question: where it is a matter of gain only a remoter fear can be enlisted to aid calculation, and a heavy inertia exists to dampen its schemes.[23]

So much depends on this insight into psychology:

> A rich and happy country like America will not stake much for the hypothetical advantages of increasing its sphere of power. ... A revisionist policy likely to incur serious costs, even in the form of conventional warfare, would be difficult for a prosperous democracy to contemplate. ... A revisionist policy backed solely by the power of a nuclear strike would surely be possible only in a pathological state of political opinion.[24]

Not content with this powerful insight into American motivations, Coral then applied it to the Soviet Union's. While conceding that Moscow was status quo-oriented in relation to its sphere of power in Eastern Europe, she argued that 'Russian power is, in aspiration, revisionist *a l'outrance* [in seeking] not only an ultimate total remaking of the power map of the world but a transformation of the nature of the whole society of states'.[25] Moscow had discovered during the Suez Crisis, she argued, that by backing revolutionary urges in the Third World, it could invest in a revisionist policy with little threat to its status quo interests in Eastern Europe: 'So there is a sense in which it can be said that the

20   ibid., pp. 199–200.
21   ibid., p. 202.
22   Daniel Kahneman and Amos Tversky, 'Prospect Theory: An Analysis of Decision Making Under Risk', *Econometrica*, vol. 47, no. 2, March 1979, pp. 263–291.
23   Bell, *Negotiation From Strength*, p. 202.
24   ibid., p. 202.
25   ibid., p. 203.

Russians have been able to use their air-atomic power as psychological backing for revisionist political objectives'.[26] Ever on the outlook for the telling *bon mot*, one can sense Coral's delight when she came across Khruschev's quote in a Walter Lippmann interview that 'the revolution is the status quo'.[27]

Two further complications add to the psychological disadvantage of the West in the competition with the Soviet bloc. The first is military technology, which has constricted decision parameters and response options: 'the revolution in military technology has operated to displace status quo by revisionist intentions at a moment of crisis, since the military operations logically required merely to ensure national survival have become identical with those required by the most sweeping revisionism'.[28] The second is the psychological effects of self- and other-images widespread among Americans:

> [T]he rather flattering and unrealistic persona that western opinion … constructs of its own character in international dealings—an essentially law-oriented, reasonable, even idealistic self-image—is not compatible with the degree of ruthlessness implied [by negotiation from strength]. Whereas the qualities we impute to the Russians, especially their alleged disregard for the human costs, even within Russia, is entirely compatible. Thus the West tends to be hoist with its own psychological warriors' petard: the Cold War image of Russian society, constructed with some deliberation in the West, becomes in itself a means of diplomatic leverage to the Russians.[29]

A Game of Shifting Momentums

Whether discussing democratic passions, alliance politics or the complexities of competitive psychology, the hydrographic metaphor of momentum seemed never far from Coral Bell's elbow. She talked from a very early stage about the shift in momentum within NATO from the United States to Europe, just as she observed Moscow's pragmatic tilt behind the momentum of Third World radicalism and Western defensiveness. And it was a hydrographic sense of advantage and disadvantage that fired her implacable conviction of the folly of the Vietnam War. The war in Vietnam was for her a 'painful and damaging misapplication of the strategy' of containment: 'The metaphor [for containment] always used, from the earliest days, was that of a dam, holding back relentless pressure. But

---

26   ibid., p. 205.
27   ibid., p. 204.
28   ibid., p. 205.
29   ibid., pp. 212–213.

what use is a dam if it is built on sand?'[30] The conditions that existed in Vietnam, which were apparent at the time, meant 'the "dam of containment" was always built on sand: politically, morally, militarily, even legally'.[31]

Coral's critique of the Vietnam War offers a clue to her understanding of containment as a grand strategy of the Cold War. Containment was never about building a perimeter fence around the extent of world communism, but rather was about identifying and fortifying a set of points of strength to be prosecuted consistently.[32] For Coral, strategy within containment must be based on a careful calculation of the balance-of-momentum: to make a stand at a point where the momentum is against you will result in a much more significant setback than just a tactical defeat. The hydrographic nature of the struggle meant that regional defeats like that in Vietnam could turn the momentum against the West in the central balance against the Soviet bloc.

It was unsurprising, then, that when Coral Bell looked back from the mid-1990s on the Cold War that had ended, that she relied heavily on a hydrographic metaphor of shifting advantage and disadvantage to tell the story of what happened.[33] The first decade was defined by rapidly oscillating initiative on either side of Eurasia—first in Berlin, then in Korea. The second decade saw the Soviet bloc gain the initiative, particularly among the revolutionary forces in the Third World. The third decade saw the initiative flow back to the peripheries of the Western alliance through the economic ascendancy of Germany and Japan. This showed the apparent Soviet momentum to be hollow, by demonstrating that war-devastated capitalist economies were comprehensively out-performing their war-devastated communist counterparts. The fourth decade saw the momentum continue to shift towards the West despite what appeared on the surface to be a losing streak between 1965 and 1980; while the fifth decade saw the Soviet Union unravel as it desperately tried to rebalance the strategic momentum against it.

For Coral Bell, momentum was about structure and agency. There were some elements of momentum that just happened as a consequence of the forces of history: one example is the rise of Third World radicalism in the 1950s and 1960s; another is the outbreak of revolutionary Islam in the 1970s and 1980s. But momentum for Coral—like *fortuna* for Machiavelli—is a force that needs to be understood and manipulated with wisdom and courage, lest it lead to ruin. To Coral's mind, Stalin and Khruschev made crucial errors in overplaying their hands when they thought momentum was with them. Stalin's obduracy led to a

30   Bell, *The Cold War in Retrospect*, p. 8.
31   ibid., p. 9.
32   John Lewis Gaddis, *Strategies of Containment: A Critical Appraisal of Postwar American National Security Policy*, Oxford University Press, Oxford, 1982.
33   Bell, *The Cold War in Retrospect*.

tightening of the NATO alliance that would never have occurred without him;[34] while Khruschev's cocksure shoe-pounding led Third World leaders to make ever more aggressive moves emboldened by the prospect of Soviet air support that never quite showed up.[35] In the end, it was a B-grade actor's sense of timing, messaging and proportion that harnessed building momentum without over-playing it, that brought an astonishingly sudden and peaceful end to the confrontation.[36]

Power Versus Values

The presidencies of Jimmy Carter and Ronald Reagan stimulated in Coral Bell an interest in values as means and ends in the Cold War. Prior to the late 1970s and 1980s, the ideological aspect of the Cold War had interested her only insofar as they affected the power and resolve of the two sides. Thus democracy, while no doubt an important system of values for Coral personally, was for a long time of scholarly interest only in terms of how it affected the West's capacity to act decisively and direct resources to strategic ends. Or when self-images of constitutionalism and moderation led to a psychological disadvantage in strategic manoeuver vis-à-vis an opponent depicted as authoritarian and deaf to the suffering of its own people.

But in Carter and Reagan the Cold War gained two primary protagonists who insisted at putting values to the fore. It was Carter and Reagan that brought to the fore the fact that the Cold War was a conflict played out on two planes—one between power systems, the other between values systems.[37] Coral found the similarities between the two administrations as intriguing as their differences. In the end she judged the Reagan team's 'right-wing Utopianism' to be the mirror image of the Carter administration's 'left-liberal Utopianism'.[38] She was particularly intrigued that many of the neo-cons who became Reagan's early cheer squad had begun their political lives on the radical left.

Ultimately, however, there is little doubt that Coral Bell saw the power conflict as the primary contest, the values conflict as secondary. Despite the rising emphasis on values in the West, on both the right and left, 'the maintenance of the Western value-system, which proposes those ideals among others [that is, human rights, development], depends in the last analysis on the maintenance of its power-position vis-à-vis adversaries proposing alternate values systems'.[39]

---

34 ibid., p. 17.
35 Bell, *Negotiation from Strength*, p. 213.
36 Bell, *The Reagan Paradox*.
37 Bell, *President Carter's Foreign Policy*, p. 100.
38 Bell, *The Reagan Paradox*, p. 139.
39 Bell, *President Carter's Foreign Policy*, p. 2.

For Coral, Kissinger had prioritised the power contest over the values contest to great effect—including for the West's cause in the contest of values, as enshrined in the Helsinki Final Act.[40] Carter prioritised value-system conflict and ended up losing on both planes. On the power-plane, while an emboldened Soviet Union went on the offensive in the Americas, Asia and Africa, the West lost crucial allies in Iran and Ethiopia. On the values-plane Carter found himself forced into a range of compromising choices, including upholding the Khmer Rouge's right to Cambodia's seat at the United Nations.[41] Reagan too found values to be a cruel mistress, leading him to embarrassment in Iran and Nicaragua.[42]

Ultimately, Coral believed values were a dangerous commodity as an ends or a means in the Cold War. Power is cold and passionless; conflicts over power can be divided, bargained, negotiated. 'Value-oriented foreign policy', on the other hand, 'usually tends to make international relations more abrasive than a power-oriented diplomacy, because on the whole it is more difficult to compromise values than to divide or offset power'.[43] In the rise of Khomeini, Coral could foresee a post-ideological age of values conflict, centred around religion and cultures. She wondered about the consequences of the possible rise of Indian, Japanese and African value systems driven by the same intensity as Khomeini's Iranian revolution, for the future of world order.

For Coral, the discussion of power came easier than the discussion of values. It was as if power was a more workable medium for her mind. Perhaps her most acute encapsulation of the grand strategies of the Cold War came in the midst of her discussion of one of the most values-driven American administrations:

> All recent Administrations in Washington have had in essence two basic tasks in international politics. First, managing the adversary relationship with the Soviet Union so that it produces neither war nor Soviet victory without war; and secondly, managing a set of relationships with the rest of the world which have inescapably become those of reduced US paramountcy.[44]

She could have easily extended the same analysis to the strategic goals of the Soviet Union, and thereby neatly summarised the whole of the Cold War.

---

40 Bell, *The Diplomacy of Détente*.
41 Bell, *President Carter's Foreign Policy*, p. 93.
42 Bell, *The Reagan Paradox*.
43 Bell, *President Carter's Foreign Policy*, p. 100.
44 Bell, *The Reagan Paradox*, p. 141.

Words Versus Actions

The Reagan Paradox is to my reading the most systematic of Coral Bell's analyses. It begins with an analytical framework that contrasts declaratory policy from operational policy, a distinction that was suggested to her by an article written by Paul Nitze on the foreign policy of John Foster Dulles in the 1950s. Both declaratory signalling—the spoken intent of a government—and operational signalling—the actual actions of a government—are important in the strategic dialogue that occurs between adversaries and allies. Although she plainly sees operational policy as the real thing (she re-uses a French adage that 'the soup is never eaten as hot as it is cooked' to observe, 'The hot soup of declaratory policy ... is necessarily cooled a bit by the breath of pragmatism before it is served as policy'[45]), she is clearly intrigued by the real-world effects of declaratory signalling. While the focus on declaratory signalling by the Reagan administration is explicit, it is by no means the first time it caught Coral's attention. As far back as *Negotiation From Strength* she was intrigued at the real strategic payoffs that accrued to the Soviet Union in the Third World from its sabre-rattling during the Suez Crisis.[46]

Coral argued that both declaratory and operational signalling were crucial to the Cold War's dynamics because they informed the expectations that each side had of the other, which in turn were incorporated into assessments of the costs and risks that informed the policy decisions of each side. More specifically, operational and declaratory signals provided the best impression of each side of the other's will. This was even more the case in the dawning 'age of surveillance' of the 1970s and 1980s, because 'the remaining ambiguities of the power balance are mostly in the area of will rather than capacity, and declaratory signals tend to determine the image of will which each group of adversary decision-makers forms of the other'.[47]

The distinction between declaratory and operational signalling was used by Coral to explain the paradoxical success of the Reagan administration in bringing on the reforms in the Soviet Union that eventually led to its collapse. She argued that it was Reagan's uncompromising declaratory signalling, from his quips about the next world war to his 'evil empire' rhetoric, that forced Moscow into a strategic corner, unable to compete and unwilling to concede. On the other hand, Reagan's mild and conciliatory operational signalling prevented the competition from boiling over into open confrontation, and prepared the ground for a new and terminal period of détente. Ultimately, the most effective declaratory signal was the 'Star Wars' missile defence program, which Coral argued the Soviets

---

45   ibid., p. 7.
46   Bell, *Negotiation from Strength*, pp. 204–205.
47   Bell, *The Reagan Paradox*, p. 23.

over-interpreted thanks to their own defence doctrine: 'Soviet standard military doctrine teaches that a strategic defensive move must be linked with a strategic offensive concept to conduce to victory. Therefore, Soviet analysts were more likely than Western ones to see a coherent strategic offensive design behind the defensive shield President Reagan kept talking of'.[48]

Ultimately, Coral's analysis of the differential effects of Reagan's words and deeds on Soviet calculations is unconvincing. It is hard to see why a confrontation-seasoned Politburo would have been simultaneously calmed by mild operational signalling while at the same time panicked by Reagan's tough-guy declaratory rhetoric. But even if one is unconvinced of her specific argument, it remains that one is still greatly enriched in having followed her reasoning and been challenged by her insights.

The Cold War as a Stage

Ultimately, it is impossible to read Coral Bell's writing on the Cold War and not be beguiled by the cast of characters she assembles: the wise, the cunning, the gormless, the bombasts. Perhaps the most persistent theme of her Cold War writing was to see that overarching conflict as a crucible in which policy-makers' character, judgement, luck and guile were put to the test. There are glimpses of consideration of structural forces in her work; she admits that 'the comparative quiet of the first Reagan term could have been seen as a natural consequence of Soviet activism in the Carter years. Reagan, in other words, then enjoyed the good fortune of Carter's bad fortune'.[49] But these are just glimpses. For Coral Bell the Cold War was ultimately a Shakespearean test of the mettle of statesmen.

Coral is as pitiless at assigning blame as she is generous in giving credit. Thus Stalin emerges repeatedly as the great bungler, overreaching in Europe and Korea and ensuring an implacable Western alliance and an isolated and increasingly weak Soviet bloc that will lose the Cold War. Repeatedly she wonders what would have happened had Stalin, rather than Roosevelt, died in 1945. On the other hand, there are those she admires. Ernest Bevin joins Kennan, Acheson, Dulles and Kissinger as the wise strategists who charted the West's course through the conflict. She is much less kind to the members of the Carter and Reagan administrations; in the end the positive momentum established by both appears more the result of Soviet over-reach than an American Svengali.

Despite her attention to the hard politics and strategic choices of the Cold War, Coral Bell was always attentive to the winners and losers. Repeatedly she asks

---

48   ibid., p. 35.
49   ibid., p. 53.

who won and who lost from a particular passage of the confrontation. Winners and losers could be alliance systems or countries; at other times she was very attentive to the women of Iran under the Khomeinist revolution. It was these considerations that bring home the fact that for Coral Bell the Cold War was always a personal, human consideration. It was probably a conviction that began as the confrontation started, in one of those ten rooms in West Block.

11. Coral Bell and the Conventions of Crisis Management

Robert Ayson

There aren't many deep works of international relations theory in the short bibliography at the end of Coral Bell's 1972 book *The Conventions of Crisis*.[1] Perhaps the most theoretically demanding are Oran Young's two books on the role of third parties and bargaining in crises. There is one book on strategic theory, Herman Kahn's masterfully unusual *On Escalation* as well as William Kaufman's study of *The McNamara Strategy*. Of the remaining entries several consist of approachable works on the evolution of international politics, including EH Carr's famous work on *The Twenty Years Crisis*, Walter Lippmann's short early study of *The Cold War* and AJP Taylor's popular history of the *Origins of the Second World War*. Perhaps most significantly of all there are three memoirs from leading American foreign policy makers: the memoirs of Dean Acheson and George Kennan and also Robert Kennedy's recollection of the 1962 Cuban Missile Crisis.

The reader might think that the contents of Bell's bibliography were simply a consequence of timing. Still to come, for example, were the big debates between the neo-realists and neo-liberals which would trap generations of students in a powerful but often lifeless intellectual universe. But I don't think that timing explains it at all. Bell's work belonged to that set of writing which concerned itself with the ideas that could be gleaned from the practice of international diplomacy. That made her more of a commentator than a theorist, but an exceptionally adroit commentator at that.

This initial judgment relies partly on personal experience. I don't actually have strong memories at all of the first time I heard Coral Bell speak. I wish I did, because the subject she was asked to lecture on as part of the core strategic studies course I was taking at The Australian National University (ANU) in 1988 was none other than 'Crisis Diplomacy'. But I do remember in that same year repeated instances of spotting the author of *The Conventions of Crisis* very much at home in the Department of International Relations Reading Room which in those days received copies of what I think was Bell's main source of daily inspiration. This was not *International Organization* or *International Security*, and certainly not the often brutally quantitative *International Studies Quarterly*

---

1   See Coral Bell, *The Conventions of Crisis: A Study in Diplomatic Management*, Oxford University Press for the Royal Institute of International Affairs, London and New York, 1971, p. 125.

all of which were held in bound volumes. It was not even the more approachable British journal *International Affairs*. It was instead a daily publication, *The International Herald Tribune*, a newspaper kept on racks in that room in the HC Coombs Building and which Bell digested each morning along with a mug of tea and an obligatory biscuit.

This *International Herald Tribune* habit (stronger perhaps than most other addictions known to modern science and even to The Australian National University) was purposeful. Bell was a close student of the interactions between the major powers of the day which in those closing years of the 1980s dealt with the last phases of the Cold War. Reading the latest American pronouncements on foreign policy, watching the reports of the meetings between Soviet and American leaders, and seeing how the increasingly less significant European leaders and the increasingly important Asian leaders were responding, revealed important ingredients for Bell's assessments. This became especially interesting when the occasional crisis would still occur in these relations.

Rather than imposing theoretical straitjackets onto international politics, Coral Bell's approach was to let the record of the practice of modern international relations gently indicate patterns of behaviour which illustrated the workings of the system of sovereign states: 'the results of a piece of crisis management', she argues, 'can only be observed in history, not established by theory. That does not mean that no theory is possible: only that theory is the stepchild of the activity, rather than its parent'.[2] The footnote to this passage underlines Bell's aversion to formal modelling, a characteristic noticeable among nearly all the contributors to the discussions of the British Committee on the Theory of International Politics, of which she was already a member: 'techniques like game theory, content analysis, operational research, systems analysis, and simulation theory already have been in use for long enough to have demonstrated their limitations as well as their occasional (and marginal) usefulness.'[3]

That aversion to formality, a common characteristic among those scholars who were influenced by Martin Wight, was also evident in Bell's assessment of the foundations of crisis management. 'I shall be preoccupied with conventions rather than rules, laws, theories, or institutions' she advises her readers, 'because these more ambitious concepts have not seemed to show much advantage in the situations I have examined.' And, in a blow for the true believers in global governance via organisational endeavour, she continues this passage with the judgement that 'Formal institutions like the UN have only been marginally and occasionally useful; many of the more successful modes of management have been strikingly non-legal, even anti-legal in quality; moral considerations

---

2   ibid., p. 6.
3   ibid., p. 6, n4.

have been no more decisive than legal ones, theory has been less apparent than intuition.' This helps to explain the rather selective bibliography alluded to above. But what then was crisis management to rely on: what approaches could possibly be left to utilise? The end of this same paragraph in the second page of the book reveals Bell's answer: 'What has emerged is the growth of conventions—I use this term in the normal sense of a practice based on tacit expectation as to what is "understood behaviour", of no special moral or legal sanctity, in a particular society'.[4]

The idea of a convention or pattern of behaviour which if shared could constitute a tacit (rather than an explicit or formal) agreement is not uncommonly found in the work of another British Committee member, Hedley Bull. But it is not his line: the inspiration comes from Thomas Schelling, a significant contributor to the argument that order in modern international politics depended upon informal agreements much more often than formal government. In the British end of this discussion (for Schelling was an American and, unlike Bell's favourite trans-Atlantic scholars, someone who used game theory to explain his arguments), the main contribution would come five years later with Bull's *The Anarchical Society*.[5] In that text, Bull argues that there is a series of institutions which provide a semblance of order for the international society of sovereign states. As we have already seen, Bell argues that her approach favours conventions over institutions, but it is not quite clear that these are mutually exclusive options.

Of the five such institutions posited by Hedley Bull, only one, international law, can be excluded from our analysis and unless I am mistaken, makes little appearance in Bell's work as a whole. But the other four all play a part, both in *Conventions* as a book and in Bell's work more generally. The first is diplomacy. Here rather than grab this institution holus bolus, Bell indicates she has identified a particular gap that needs to be filled by the present study: 'Undoubtedly crisis management should be considered just a special skill within the general field of diplomacy. ... Diplomatic history recounts many such crises, but does not generalize about crisis as such'.[6] And yet the remainder of the volume makes so many references to the political interactions between the major players in international affairs, as does so much of Bell's work that it is undeniable that diplomacy is at the forefront.

But as with the rest of her work, Bell is not just interested in diplomacy between any old set of countries. Her focus, she announces, will be squarely on the interactions between the 'dominant powers' which she defines as the 'the powers that move and shake the world' of which at present there were 'only

---

4 ibid., p. 2.
5 Hedley Bull, *The Anarchical Society: A Study of Order in World Politics*, Macmillan, Basingstoke, 1977.
6 Bell, *The Conventions of Crisis*, p. 4.

three—America, Russia and China.' Bell excludes Japan from this list; it belongs in her view to the wider grouping of great powers, a 'traditional term' which she chooses not to use.[7] But that she then suggests that there were seven such 'dominant powers' in the interwar years; 'Germany, Britain, France, America, Russia, Japan, and Italy' indicates that she is indeed talking about the great powers, which comprise another one of Bull's five institutions for international order.

As the movers and shakers, it is the dominant powers which have the unique ability to turn local crises into central ones, a facility whose importance grows because of a relatively new ingredient in their relations: the arrival of nuclear weapons. Hence Bell's argument that she will be 'preoccupied with crises affecting the powers of the central nuclear balance, because the policy choices of their decision-makers have consequences of such gravity.'[8] That explains the omission of 'great power' Japan, whose lack of nuclear weapons Hedley Bull sometimes argued denied it a place in even that category. And it offers a connection to the two other institutions that feature in Bull's anarchical international society. One, mentioned discreetly in this passage is the balance of power, which in the Cold War often became synonymous with the nuclear balance. Bell suggests to her readers that she has already dealt with the question in her earlier book, *Negotiation from Strength,* one of many studies she says had been devoted to the question of 'the stabilization of the central balance of power'.[9] But this feature of contemporary international relations still acts as the background issue for almost all that is to come in *Conventions.*

Why that should be the case is revealed by the last of Hedley Bull's institutions which is war. It may seem nonsensical that in an age of nuclear armaments, war could be part of the management of any crisis, for surely it would mean the end of everything. But Coral Bell for one did not believe that as a genus, war had been made extinct in the nuclear age: 'War as an institution flourishes as robustly as ever it did: there have been about eighty sets of armed encounters of an identifiable sort in what is usually called the post-war period'.[10] Slightly earlier she notes her agreement with the argument that 'The propensity to conflict must be accepted as a continuing fact of human life, even though, among nations, the technical means for pursuing conflicts are now so monstrously efficient as to threaten the end of human life itself.'[11] And this dual fact—the ubiquity of war and the hazards of its most potent form—explained the point and purpose of crisis management. This was not an art designed to remove crises, let alone war in totality. Because that might be called crisis elimination. It was to manage

---

7   ibid., p. 7.
8   ibid., p. 7.
9   ibid., p. 1.
10 ibid., p. 5.
11 ibid., p. 6.

the situation in such a way that local brushfires did not, through the careless involvement of the dominant powers, become all-out infernos. In that sense crisis management was akin to the arms control logic that both Schelling and Bull had outlined a decade before whose job was to effect restraint in conflict rather than its avoidance.[12] As Bell herself argued, 'A sense of the permanence of conflict, and the probability of crisis, between nations is the only adequate incentive to serious work on managing crises and limiting the destructiveness of the armed hostilities they make evoke'.[13]

Here Bell was contributing to a tradition of thinking that the international system did not suddenly grind to a halt as soon as force was used: diplomacy did not stop as soon as the firing started, but could continue into it. However, now that nuclear weapons were on the scene, the appearance of catastrophic war would be a sign that the management of this state system had failed. To study the management of crises was therefore to study the crisis points, decision points or turning points (terms Bell uses) between the conflict situations which were only to be expected and the catastrophes which had to be avoided. And it was a particular turning point, which fortunately had gone the right way, that was responsible for the rise of the art of crisis management: the Cuban Missile Crisis. The conscious effort to maintain a stable balance (as opposed to the more or less accidental turn of events beforehand—also observed by Bull) had been more noticeable since 1962, and thus *The Conventions of Crisis* is its record over the first decade of practice.

At the risk of artificially reducing her work to a single focus, it might therefore be said that Coral Bell's main interest was the way that the practice of a special form of diplomacy manages the central balance between the great powers so as to preclude the catastrophic war that would end the inevitably conflict-ridden system of states. If there is any doubt that Bell's focus here is the avoidance of Armageddon and not the promotion of universal peace, that uncertainty goes away immediately when in the first paragraph of *The Conventions of Crisis* Coral Bell asks:

> [H]ow is it that peace has been preserved since 1945? What are the modes of behaviour which have prevented the endemic crises of the postwar period from turning into central wars? (I speak of central war because limited and peripheral wars have been a fairly constant feature of the time).[14]

---

12   The author considers these in *Thomas Schelling and the Nuclear Age: Strategy as Social Science*, Frank Cass, London, 2004 and *Hedley Bull and the Accommodation of Power*, Palgrave Macmillan, Basingstoke, 2012.
13   Bell, *The Conventions of Crisis*, p. 6.
14   ibid., p. 1.

Crisis Management not Problem Solving

Coral Bell had an unsettling habit of proffering rather innocuous and roundabout examples of the very serious practices of international relations that she was writing about. She does this by giving as an example of a convention, 'the taboo on eating peas from one's knife.'[15] And she also invents some rather genteel metaphors—the crisis slide when multiple tensions produce a cumulative effect, as in the years immediately preceding the First and Second World Wars, and alternatively the placement of a second crisis on the 'backburner' while the first was being dealt with, an approach which she argues was applied to the Laos crisis of the early 1960s when there was already a major crisis occurring in nearby Vietnam.[16] I'm not sure whether these metaphors did more to obscure or illustrate the deadly serious points Bell was making. But the second of them is a reflection of the philosophy that she took to her subject while the first is an indication of her objective.

There was absolutely nothing wrong in Bell's view with the backburner strategy. In fact there was a lot to be said for it. Sometimes the attempt to address a crisis head-on could be counterproductive, and that risk was multiplied if the intent was to resolve it. When the cause of a crisis is especially intractable, and here Bell uses the ongoing example of the contest between Greece and Turkey for Cyprus, any hope of a real solution only rests with fools. In such conflicts: 'No diplomatic formula is going to make them disappear: they have to be lived with'.[17] In that knowledge, the dominant powers needed to be extremely cautious about getting involved, and needed to resist the temptation of dreaming that they could be successful mediators. Bell notes that in this particular case, a series of leading American leaders had tried, including Dean Acheson and Cyrus Vance, but she offers the following warning: 'If people assume that these mediators have failed, it is because they do not distinguish between crisis management and conflict resolution. They expect crisis management to "solve" the Cyprus situation in some magical fashion'.[18]

Crisis management was not about solving the problem at the root of the crisis, it was about ensuring that the crisis did not get worse—or amalgamate with other crises into the crisis slide that had preceded catastrophic conflict twice already in the twentieth century. A crisis manager was a person who helped their country survive the massive test that a crisis could pose to a relationship—this could be a relationship between opposing dominant powers where the risk was a passage from peace into war, or it could be an 'intramural' relationship within

---

15   ibid., p. 2.
16   ibid., pp. 19, 90.
17   ibid., p. 93.
18   ibid., p. 93.

an alliance where the risk was an alliance rupture. 'To my mind', writes Bell early on in the book, 'the essence of a true crisis in any given relationship is that the conflicts within it rise to a level which threatens to transform the nature of the relationship'.[19]

This meant that Bell was no enemy of the status quo in international politics, so long as that status quo was not full of dominant powers who sought to revolutionise the basis of their relations with one another. She had concerns that of her three dominant powers China, which had not properly escaped the Cultural Revolution, but which had an earlier history of more cautious behaviour, remained a revisionist actor on the international scene. But as she was writing her book in between Henry Kissinger's visit to China and the subsequent trip to see Mao that President Nixon would lead, Bell thought that 'the process of establishment of tacit understandings, already far advanced between America and Russia, appeared to be developing surprisingly fast between America and China'.[20] Moreover even if China was to misbehave, it would be outweighed by the preponderance of power which 'for a long time to come is likely to rest with the tacit understanding between the USA and the Soviet Union. And this I regard as conducive to peace'.[21]

In fact Bell went as far to suggest that this preponderance was reminiscent of the European Concert[22] which, in siding with the generous view (and in omitting the mid-nineteenth century wars in Crimea and western Europe) she saw as responsible for keeping the peace for the best part of the century. The European Concert thus becomes under Bell's treatment a long-lasting crisis management arrangement. This point of comparison confirms her preference for the status quo and for the notion that order rests with the interactions of an elite group of great powers. In those tea and biscuit sessions in the Coombs Building with the *International Herald Tribune*, I suspect she was considering whether the leaders of the day were measuring up to the standards of Metternich and Castlereagh.

But unlike their European predecessors (whose record was trampled in the first half of the twentieth century), Bell thought that the crisis managers of the dominant powers in the post-war era had some inbuilt advantages. Hedley Bull, who also harked back at times to the record of the Concert, would have called these accidents of history. One was the arrival of nuclear weapons and the mutual deterrence that in significant numbers they provided for. Almost undoubtedly borrowing an idea from Thomas Schelling (to whom she refers a little later in the book), Bell argues that the relationship between the Soviet Union and the United States can be characterised as a massive 'exchange of

---

19 ibid., p. 9.
20 ibid., p. 122.
21 ibid., p. 68.
22 ibid., p. 69.

hostages'.[23] This mutual vulnerability provided a constant reminder of the need to show restraint in times of crisis. That restraint in turn was made more plausible by another child of modern military technology: the knowledge of one another's military capabilities that advanced systems of surveillance provided. This made it less likely for crisis slides to be encouraged by either an exaggeration or underestimation of the capabilities held by a potential combatant. Just as Britain's underestimation of Soviet capabilities before the Second World War had reduced London's view of the value that an alliance with Moscow might bring, in Bell's view its exaggeration of German capabilities had also led to the crisis slide towards the events of 1939.[24] That was now less likely.

But crisis management was a conscious process. It did not occur accidentally thanks to new technology and to what others had called the balance of terror. Perhaps the biggest advantage the major participants in the Cold War had over their First and Second World War equivalents was their early admission that their relationship was in fact an adversarial one. Like members of the local branch of the Alcoholics Anonymous, their acceptance of the problem was the foundation for hope that things could improve. For Bell this admission had come as early as 1946, and it was certainly there in the Truman Doctrine of the following year.[25] With that early recognition comes hope that in the early stages of their Cold War relationship the Russians and Americans were aware of the things that divided them.

But that itself gave no guarantee that they would work together in what Bell calls an 'adverse partnership', a term she borrows from the American specialist on Soviet affairs Marshall Shulman. That partnership would not reflect the notion that the dominant powers enjoyed a relationship that was 'particularly cordial, trusting, or friendly'. Instead, in words that again evoke Schelling (and his main interpreter for British audiences Hedley Bull), Bell depicts the partnership as consisting of a 'consciousness between the dominant powers, that they have solid common interests as well as sharp conflicting interests'.[26] And it had taken the crisis of all Cold War crises, the one in Cuba, to get the two main dominant powers fully aware of their need to manage the relationship they had with one another.

---

23   ibid., p. 52.
24   ibid., pp. 56–57.
25   ibid., pp. 21–24.
26   ibid., p. 50.

Signalling not Fighting?

How then would the dominant powers conduct that crisis management? What would be their weapons of choice? That second question is asked as a teaser, because the costs of direct war between the dominant powers were so great that it might seem that armed forces had become redundant. Indeed Bell herself offers an opinion in the later stages of the book that crisis may eventually take the place of war as a mechanism for change. Indeed a crisis, if 'properly managed ... may ultimately enable states to write their peace treaties without first fighting the war'.[27] That makes crisis management the friend of the status quo in terms of the absence of a breakdown in peace. It also makes it a colleague of the presence of peaceful change.

But it does not mean that questions of force have been removed from the picture. Bell's nominee for the main mechanism for crisis management is the signal, and many of these signals have as their subject the role of armed force in the adversarial partnership. Again the arguments of Schelling seems to be rather to the front of Bell's mind: 'the basic instrument of crisis management', she advises her readers, 'is what I shall call the signal.' (She was not alone in doing that). And 'By signal I mean a threat or offer communicated to the other party or parties to the crisis'.[28] In the threat side of that signalling register, Bell admits later on (and now with citations of Schelling's opinions) that crisis management relies heavily on coercion.[29] Her defence that especially in an era of nuclear weapons, coercion may be 'the least of a number of evils'[30] confirms that her eye is on the practicable and not the perfectable.

What sort of coercion then does Bell rely on? Not for her are economic sanctions of which she has a low opinion.[31] She sticks to her guns: 'Some of the sharpest and most effective [signals] are movements of military resources of various sorts'.[32] Even the limited use of force can act as a potent form of communication: 'Border hostilities themselves are a kind of signal'.[33] This is Schelling's diplomacy of violence,[34] delivered in a more historically and politically aware fashion. Similar too is Bell's argument that the adverse partnership between the Soviet Union and United States was based in part on a 'common strategic ideology' which included a 'tacit consensus' on how particular weapons systems should

---

27   ibid., p. 116.
28   ibid., p. 73.
29   ibid., pp. 100–101.
30   ibid., p. 100.
31   ibid., p. 77.
32   ibid., p. 73.
33   ibid., p. 74.
34   See Thomas C. Schelling, *Arms and Influence*, Yale University Press, New Haven, 1966.

be understood and a 'tacit understanding' of how they might be employed.[35] Bell also speaks of a stabilising commonality in thinking brought on by an exchange of ideas across the Iron Curtain: 'if you ask who is the Soviet version of Schelling or Kahn or Wohlstetter, the answer is probably Schelling or Kahn or Wohlstetter, even though the doctrine may be mediated through Sokolovsky or Talensky or Rotmistrov.'[36]

This is just the sort of statement that would cause the analysts of Soviet strategic culture, who would soon be publishing their research,[37] to have kittens. In portraying this extent of symmetry in Soviet–American strategic behaviour Bell may have been getting beyond what the evidence would support, although she was by no means alone in doing so. What is striking is that she holds to these views of strategic communication and signalling in the early 1970s by which time America's experience in Vietnam had dealt this style of reasoning a blow from which it would never completely recover. This does not mean that signalling has become obsolete as a strategic practice: it is all too evident (and not necessarily in the service of a partnership) in China–US interactions in Asia today. But after Vietnam confidence in exploiting what Schelling famously called the power to hurt dropped markedly (by which time his own work was exploring different subjects).

It is doubly interesting that Coral Bell stuck with this view even though she too held Vietnam to be an unmitigated tragedy for American policy and as such the most obvious reminder that intervention 'in the civil wars of minor powers' is a practice that dominant powers should 'avoid at all costs'.[38] Vietnam stood as a costly failure in crisis management above all because 'the decision-makers concerned did not keep sight of their first principle: that political ends should maintain ascendancy over military means in crisis decision-making'.[39] (Crisis managers needed to be good Clausewitzians). That danger had been aggravated by another technological innovation, the advent of the 'television "global village"' thanks to which 'domestic revulsion against a remote war has certainly never before in history been as politically effective as it has been in America over the Vietnam War'.[40] Bell thought this disjuncture so serious (and so paralysing) that 'Western participation in counter-insurgency operations must in future be ruled out as unfeasible for domestic political reasons, unless the moral case is absolutely watertight, which it seldom is in international politics'.[41] This bears some reflection in 2014 as the West comes out of another period of intervention

---

35   Bell, *The Conventions of Crisis*, pp. 59–60.
36   ibid., p. 61.
37   For the leading example, see Jack Snyder, *The Soviet Strategic Culture: Implications for Nuclear Options*, R- 2154-AF, Rand Corporation, Santa Monica, 1977.
38   Bell, *The Conventions of Crisis*, pp. 107–108.
39   ibid., p. 109.
40   ibid., p. 104–105.
41   ibid., p. 105.

(this time in Iraq and Afghanistan). It is also intriguing against the findings of a striking new study of contemporary war, *War from the Ground Up*, which argues that the spread of information technology (the social media variant of the 'global village') brings forth a multitude of new audiences to whom strategic messages must be communicated effectively. But unlike Bell, this new book posits this as a reminder of how war needs to be waged rather than as a prime reason for its avoidance.[42] I think on this question my money is with the author of *The Conventions of Crisis*.

Conclusion: Strategic Elitism?

Instead of war from the ground up, Bell's work is clearly a case of the diplomacy of crisis management from the top down. Her view of international order relies almost completely on a small elite of decision-makers in each of the very small number of dominant powers, the United States, Russia and China. It is the interactions within these adverse partnerships (for none of them are close pals) where the hopes for successful crisis management really rest. She does of course admit the category of intramural crisis management between allies, including the Suez Crisis of 1956, but she relegates these to secondary importance. Bell was no sentimentalist for the British Empire and its descendants in the British Commonwealth in this respect. At one point she describes Britain, India and Australia all as 'minor powers'.[43] One alliance really did matter, though. This was NATO, where the European powers, including nuclear-armed Britain and France had some sway in shaping the views and decision-making of the dominant power. But NATO was the exception to the rule. Most of the western alliances were 'like ANZUS, with the United States allied to one or two powers of small military strength and no great diplomatic leverage or experience'.[44] There were no favours for present-day advocates of Australia as a middle power here. Indeed, while most of the book was written at The Australian National University, Bell felt no need to be a spruiker for the country of her birth.

In *The Conventions of Crisis*, and I think in her other writings, Bell is part of an intellectual elite speaking to other elites, including contemporary decision-makers. Even the metaphors assume an affinity for a group of people who can speak about threats of enormous violence as if they were hands played in a calm but serious game of bridge. That possibly also helps explain the links Bell seeks to draw between the Concert of Europe and the Cold War, which on at least two occasions she says had received too much of a 'bad press', misunderstood

---

42   See Emile Simpson, *War from the Ground Up*, Hurst, London, 2012.
43   Bell, *The Conventions of Crisis*, p. 68.
44   ibid., p. 91.

as a 'prelude to hostilities rather than a substitute' for them.[45] The elitism also extends to the political actors she admits and dismisses. There is almost no sign at all (and in fact I think none at all) of non-state actors in her main study of crisis management. Later on in her career, when she admits Al-Qaeda and its ilk into her discussion of the world's strategic problems, the analytical function of the non-state actor is to provide a common point of threat which will allow a new international concert of powers to emerge against it. She was ruthlessly state-centric even in her evaluation of actors other than states. I suspect that also was a reason for her questioning of the significance of the United Nations.

Strategic elitism is not without its virtues. The notion of three dominant powers, for example, has the advantage of parsimony which some of Bell's colleagues have found very suitable in their own analysis.[46] It allowed a clarity of vision which populated many of Bell's very popular talks to students and officials. It reminded us perhaps of an age when things seemed simpler. Or perhaps it told us that we have not escaped from a time when international order depends on how well the major players manage the crises that come between them. It is when they ignore crises, and even more when they try earnestly to solve them, that we so often find ourselves in trouble. For that reason Bell's work on the conventions of crisis management deserves a contemporary audience.

45   ibid., p. 26.
46   See my analysis of Hugh White's *China Choice* in Robert Ayson, 'Is Minimal Order Enough? Hugh White's Strategic Parsimony', *Security Challenges*, vol. 9, no. 1, Autumn 2013, pp. 17–26.

12. Coral Bell's Alliance Politics: Practitioner and Pundit

William T Tow

Coral Bell was Australia's premier expert on alliance politics during and after the Cold War. Former US Secretary of State Dean Acheson's famous book title, *Present at the Creation*, applies equally to this remarkable Australian figure who was both a practitioner in and pundit on this subject.[1] She was 'in the room' as an officer with Australia's Department of External Affairs when the ANZUS (Australia New Zealand United States) Treaty was signed in San Francisco on 1 September 1951.

One of her most avid interests pursued during a subsequent and distinguished career as an academic and think-tank adviser was assessing American leadership of its global alliance system and continually evaluating how Australia fared in and should respond to Washington's strategic policies. Her book *Dependent Ally: A Study in Australian Foreign Policy* (three editions were published) remains a seminal work on how Australia—one of the United States' smaller allies—was able to calibrate its security relationship with an American superpower in ways that facilitated its maturity as an independent security actor.[2] During her later years, she became increasingly preoccupied with how the Australian–American alliance would function in a world undergoing rapid structural change and where global multipolarity and great power concerts would prevail. To what extent her viewpoints will be proven to be correct or misplaced is far less important than her success in initiating the debate about international order-building which had to take place within official policy circles, think-tanks, and academe. In commemorating her life and work soon after her passing, Owen Harries observed that 'she always tackled the great central questions of international politics … major topics [such] as the central balance, the management of crises and of great alliances, the temptations and dangers of hegemony'.[3]

Three key dimensions of Bell's work on alliance politics are discussed in this chapter. Initially, an assessment is offered on where her work fits within the evolution of alliance theory. The basic theme of this section is that she ranks among the very best of all those who have written on the subject. The second

---

1   Dean Acheson, *Present at the Creation: My Years in the State Department*, WW Norton, New York, 1969.
2   Coral Bell, *Dependent Ally: A Study in Australian Foreign Policy,* 3rd edn, Allen & Unwin, Sydney, in association with Department of International Relations, Australian National University, 1993.
3   Owen Harries, 'A Tribute to Coral Bell', *The Spectator*, 6 October 2012, www.spectator.co.uk/australia/australia-features/8643341/a-tribute-to-coral-bell/ (accessed 18 August 2013).

part of the chapter focuses on those dimensions of alliance management where her analysis was particularly incisive. Alliance leadership and power balancing were central concerns in this context. The chapter's third section reviews her quest to reconcile traditional alliance postures with the politics of concert in the twenty-first century. She fused her remarkable grasp of diplomatic history with objective thinking about how historic changes in contemporary global security relations were affecting the Western alliance system and its Australian–American component. This discussion reveals the essence of Bell's core intellectual identity and illustrates what may be her most enduring legacy.

Alliance Theory

Overcoming the challenges of managing security alliances has always represented a critical and often frustrating enterprise for policy-makers. Writing soon after the Peloponnesian War was fought over two millennia ago, Thucydides compared the advantages of states pooling their resources to deter or prevail in war against the option of pursuing or sustaining dominance over rival or rising powers.[4] The continued relevance of the analyses of this venerated Greek historian has been underscored by the American political scientist Graham Allison, who warned that China and the United States must avoid the 'Thucydides trap' of succumbing to fears about power transition if they wished to avoid destroying each other.[5] Other 'classical' strategists concerned about modern alliance politics have complemented or built upon the work of Thucydides. China's Sun Tzu, India's Kautilya (also known as Chanakya or Vishnugupta), Renaissance Italy's Niccolo Machiavelli, Prussia's Carl von Clausewitz, and Britain's EH Carr are regarded as pantheons in the field. While their individual explanations regarding exercising political power may have differed, all believed that the state was the ultimate arbitrator of how power would be applied and viewed alliances as critical instruments to achieve political objectives.[6]

In modern times, alliance formation and perpetuation have been linked to realist theories about international anarchy and power balancing. Realists have posited that in the absence of a preeminent actor to manage order, states will ally in a self-help world to either neutralise a rising threat or to 'bandwagon'

---

4   Thucydides, *History of the Peloponnesian War*, Penguin, Hammondsworth, 1972.

5   Graham Allison, 'Thucydides's Trap Has Been Sprung in the Pacific', *Financial Times*, 21 August 2012. Critics of this perspective, however, note that Sparta was criticised by its own allies for being too risk averse! See Daniel Drezner, 'The Limits of Thucydides in the 21st Century', *Foreign Policy*, 29 May 2013, drezner. foreignpolicy.com/posts/2013/05/29/the_limits_of_thucydides_in_the_21st_century (accessed 18 August 2013). The classic work on power transition theory remains AFK Organski and Jacek Kugler, *The War Ledger*, University of Chicago Press, Chicago, 1980.

6   See, for example, Roger Boesche, 'Moderate Machiavelli? Contrasting *The Prince* with the *Arthashastra* of Kautilya', *Critical Horizons*, vol. 3, no. 2, 2002, pp. 253–76.

with a benign or inexorable hegemon to avoid conquest or to accrue a share in geopolitical spoils. The writings of Hans Morgenthau, George Liska, Henry Kissinger, Robert Osgood, Glenn Snyder, Kenneth Waltz, Stephen Walt, and John Mearsheimer have been particularly associated, since the Second World War, with the development of thinking about alliances.

Writing prior to and during the 1960s, Morgenthau—the acknowledged don of modern realist thought—focused largely on why alliances form and how well they endure. A 'second wave' of alliance literature emerging in the 1970s, and spearheaded by a landmark study authored by Ole Holsti, Terrence Hopmann, and John Sullivan, was more quantitative in nature and was mainly concerned with how alliances fit within the evolving post-war international system.[7] A third wave of theoretical realist writing about alliances emerged in the 1980s, led by Kenneth Waltz, which again emphasised alliance formation but infused systemic analysis into its investigations.[8] By this time, a clear divide was discernible between those who opted to use diplomatic history as their preferred means for evaluating alliance politics in the hope that policy-makers would listen to them, and those, usually located in academic institutions, who preferred to refine and build upon a growing body of alliance theory, and were less concerned about 'real world' responses to their work. As the notable alliance theorist Walt has since observed, 'academic theory—including my own work—has had relatively little direct or indirect impact on actual state behaviour. Scholars may tell themselves they are 'speaking truth to power', but most of the time the powerful don't listen.'[9]

Bell was the exception to the rule that Walt posited. When addressing alliance politics, she demonstrated a remarkable capacity to assess the very hard problems of strategic choice for the US, Australia, and the West-at-large. She invariably conveyed her insights by elegantly referencing diplomatic history. Both the quintessential Australian Labor Party (ALP) policy practitioner (and later diplomat) Kim Beazley and the revered Australian international relations theorist James L Richardson recognised Bell's exceptional talent for combining 'real-world' analysis with highly sophisticated historical perspectives. Beazley observed that Bell's work transcended the 'mathematically quantifiable interactions' that typified International Relations (IR) theory during her prime (as reflected in the second and third waves of alliance literature cited above). Noting that she 'stood out' as one of the two premier Australian IR scholars (Hedley Bull being the other) that captured the attention of policy practitioners,

---

7 Ole R Holsti, P Terrence Hopmann, and John D Sullivan, *Unity and Disintegration in International Alliances: Comparative Studies*, Wiley, New York, 1973.

8 Kajsa Ji Noe Oest, 'The End of Alliance Theory?' Institut for Statskundskab, Copenhagen University, Copenhagen, 2007, p. 27, polsci.ku.dk/arbejdspapirer/2007/ap_2007_03.pdf/ (accessed 18 August 2013).

9 Stephen M. Walt, 'Theory and Policy in International Relations: Some Personal Reflections', *Yale Journal of International Affairs*, vol. 7, no. 2, 2012: pp. 33–43, at 35.

Beazley ventured that 'it is when scholars write in traditional, historically based terms that their influence is most felt outside the academy. I've never heard much game theory discussed by delegates to ALP National Conference but I heard, particularly in the 1980s, the more traditional writing of many here discussed ad nauseum'.[10] Richardson insisted that Bell's form of 'classical realism' stemmed from understanding of the 'fixed beliefs of decision-makers' and the constraints those individuals faced in dealing with perceived domestic political imperatives. Her approach, he concluded, constituted 'a much-needed corrective to the systemic, structural emphases in the prevailing neorealist doctrine'.[11]

Richardson's observation is particularly important in understanding the importance of Bell's interpretation of why and how the ANZUS or tripartite alliance between the United States, Australia, and New Zealand was created. As a junior officer in Australia's Ministry of External Affairs, she was actually 'present at creation' when ANZUS was signed by its three adherents in San Francisco in September 1951.[12] Her explanation of why the event she witnessed came about, and how ANZUS evolved, is offered in her much acclaimed book, *Dependent Ally*. The work remains arguably the preeminent study on Australia's post-war alliance (the other widely acclaimed study of ANZUS creation was written by JG Starke, and, while technically proficient, was written primarily as an international law treatise).[13] What separated Bell's work from that of her contemporaries (and from that of those alliance historians who followed her) was her capacity to weave her narrative in ways that captured the drama and tensions that underlay the process of alliance formation and to relate the story

---

10   Kim Beazley, 'Thinking Security: Influencing National Strategy from the Academy; An Australian Experience', Coral Bell Lecture 2008, Lowy Institute for International Policy, Sydney, 19 March 2008, p. 5. www.lowyinstitute.org/files/pubfiles/Beazley,_Thinking_security,_Vote_of_thanks.pdf (accessed 25 August 2013).

11   James L Richardson, 'Coral Bell and the Classical Realist Tradition', *Australian Journal of International Affairs*, vol. 59, no. 3, 2005, pp. 265–8, at 267–8.

12   Brendan Taylor, 'Security Cooperation in the Asia-Pacific Region', in Ron Huisken and Meredith Thatcher (eds), *History as Policy: Framing the Debate on The Future of Australia's Defence Policy*, Canberra: ANU E Press, 2007, pp. 117–128, at p. 123.

13   JG Starke, *The ANZUS Treaty Alliance*, Melbourne University Press, Melbourne,1965. Other widely cited works on ANZUS formation include Percy C Spender, *Exercises in Diplomacy: The ANZUS Treaty and the Colombo Plan*, Sydney University Press, Sydney, 1969; Glenn St J Barclay and JM Siracusa (eds), *Australian–American Relations Since 1945: A Documentary History*, Holt, Rinehart & Winston, Sydney, 1976; HC Gelber, *The Australian American Alliance: Costs and Benefits*, Penguin, Hammondsworth, 1968; TR Reese, *Australia, New Zealand and the United States: A Survey of International Relations, 1941–1968*, Royal Institute of International Affairs/Oxford University Press, London and New York, 1969; HS Albinski, *ANZUS, the United States and Pacific Security*, University Press of America, Lanham, 1987; A. Burnett (ed), *The ANZUS Documents*, Department of International Relations, The Australian National University, Canberra, 1991; and Joseph M Siracusa, 'The ANZUS Treaty Revisited', *Security Challenges*, vol. 1, no. 1, 2005, pp. 89–104.

she was telling to historical timeframes. As Beazley noted when delivering the first Lowy Institute lecture named in her honour, 'Coral Bell's work transits through contemporary writing like a permanently open time capsule'.[14]

Indeed, Bell was masterful in linking successive episodes of Western alliance behaviour to frame powerful cross-comparisons that facilitated a holistic understanding of the entire post-war order-building process. When writing about the differences between the relatively successful ANZUS and the ill-fated Southeast Asia Treaty Organization (SEATO), Bell illustratively pointed to the vital but inadequately understood dissimilarities between the two security arrangements. ANZUS was specifically designed to defend Australian sovereign territory against a direct military attack by a hostile party, initially thought to be a strategically resurgent Japan. SEATO was intended to underwrite a very different kind of policy—Australia's pursuit of a 'forward defence' strategy in Southeast Asia directed against communist insurgency movements that, if successful, might topple pro-Western or neutral governments there and isolate Australia in the process.[15] A US regional strategic presence was what Australia valued most, but Australian policy-makers often felt they were competing with their British counterparts—Britain was also a member of SEATO—for American attention and resources. This sense of competition, Bell presciently observed, may ultimately not have served either Australia or the US well.

ANZUS provided Australia with a relatively exclusive forum (only shared with New Zealand) to convey security concerns to US officials. Australia might have been better off over the long-term 'if US policy-makers had been forced to defend their Asian or Pacific policies in a forum where European voices had also to be heard, urging alternative priorities' to forward defence.[16] That such was not the case meant that the US could easily pressure Australia and New Zealand to make force contributions to an escalating conflict in Vietnam during the 1960s (without formally activating SEATO as a trigger for such involvement) even as Britain and France declined to extend material support to the Lyndon B Johnson administration for that struggle. In this context, Bell's alliance narrative beautifully illustrated the 'alliance security dilemma' and its focus on entrapment and abandonment as it applied to Southeast Asia during the Cold War. Her work in this area, coincidentally, complements Victor Cha's later application of that theoretical approach to understanding the dynamics of US alliance politics with Japan and South Korea in Northeast Asia.[17]

---

14   Beazley, 'Thinking Security', p. 1.
15   Bell, *Dependent Ally*, pp. 47–48, 68.
16   ibid., p. 46.
17   Victor D. Cha, 'Abandonment, Entrapment, and Neoclassical Realism in Asia: The United States, Japan, and Korea', *International Studies Quarterly*, vol. 44, no. 2, 2000, pp. 261–91. Cha develops a model in which Japan and South Korea are more at odds with each other when either Japan or South Korea fear that US resolve to stay committed to their own national security is weakening. In a similar vein, Bell's characterisation of Australian fears that US strategic interest in Southeast Asia would be compromised by America's apprehensions

Alliance Leadership and Power Balancing

What sets Bell's commentary apart from the aforementioned 'three waves' of international relations literature is her shrewd appreciation of 'elite identity' and policy management as a key factor—perhaps *the* key factor—in alliance politics. In Australia's case, she observed that while its national security interests have remained fairly constant, 'the personality and assumptions of Australia's chief decision-maker of any given time' was absolutely critical.[18] The dominant figure in Australian Cold War politics, Prime Minister Robert G Menzies, clearly exemplified this proposition. Initially reticent about Australia's contribution of ground forces to the Korean War due to the British Labour government's similar reticence, he learned about London's subsequent decision to commit forces (after having been pressured by the US) to that conflict only after reaching New York on one of his long sea voyages to the US and Britain. Bell's description of Menzies' *volte face* was a classic illustration of her beautifully understated representations of historical policy benchmarks:

> [Thus] confronted with a fait accompli ... he took the news of this reversal of his original injunction [not to commit Australian ground troops to UN military operations in Korea] in his stride, acquiesced in it without objection, and blandly proceeded to enjoy a considerable personal success (including the raising of a loan for Australia) during his Washington visit on the strength of his involuntary redefinition as the readiest and staunchest of the USA's friends.[19]

Bell noted that, earlier, Menzies' original scepticism about entering into a regional security treaty with the United States *sans* Britain flowed from similar concerns. Excessive dependence on an American security alliance would corner Australia into signing a Japanese peace treaty that would be unpopular with his own electorate and could undermine the Commonwealth's significance as an Asian security actor. The latter was especially true as the Emergency in the Malaya Peninsula was intensifying (a conflict in which Washington did not want its own forces to become involved) and British forces deployed there remained critical to defusing that threat.

In further exposition of Bell's appreciation of 'elite identity', she cited that negotiating ANZUS largely succeeded due to the single-minded quest of Percy Spender (who was appointed ambassador to the US when the Menzies government resumed power in mid-1951). Initial opposition by the US Joint Chiefs of Staff

---

that it would be embroiled in defending British interests there conforms to this model. Thinking on the alliance security dilemma was developed by Glenn H Snyder, 'The Security Dilemma in Alliance Politics', *World Politics*, vol. 36, no. 4, 1984, pp. 461–495.

18   Bell, *Dependent Ally*, p. 175.

19   ibid., p. 42.

to the accord weakened when Spender 'bluntly' linked Australia's willingness to support a peace treaty with Japan to 'the nature of the security arrangements arrived at for Australia'. By this time, Menzies' own position had softened as he realised that Britain was embarking on a long recessional from previous colonial responsibilities east of the Suez Canal and that Australia would be largely dependent on American power to contain Japanese remilitarisation and help underwrite Australia's 'forward defence' strategy in Southeast Asia. Spender and US Special Envoy John Foster Dulles teamed up to push the Australian agenda through a series of complex negotiations and counter-negotiations orchestrated by Winston Churchill's conservative British government which opposed an ANZUS without British membership.[20]

Bell's conclusion that Australia's security relations with the US have evolved from it being a de facto 'protectorate' involved in a 'one-way' security guarantee from Washington into a more equal arrangement as the Cold War transpired is entirely valid. The United States became increasingly dependent on the US–Australia joint installations for generating credible deterrence policy and gathering critical intelligence. Bell then made the legitimate and important observation that both countries' leaderships must be successful in ensuring that ANZUS was pursuing the 'common interest in a stable balance-of-power in the world' and that this 'outweigh[ed] any prospective divergence between particular national interests'. She noted that original alliance asymmetry had morphed into something more equal as global strategic interdependence and multipolarity intensified:

> It [ANZUS] had become considerably less unequal … in the sense that Australian dependence on the USA for protection had been narrowed to the relatively unlikely catastrophe of general war. … A one-sided dependence had in effect transmuted itself into interdependence of a relatively symmetrical sort.[21]

Historians have most often pointed to Gough Whitlam's government as the catalyst for Australia maturing into a more independent regional actor and for challenging what they viewed as the American predisposition to regard Australia as a reliably subservient ally.[22] It is clear that successive Australian conservative

---

20   ibid., pp. 43–45.

21   ibid., p. 183.

22   Among the many in-depth surveys of Australia–US relations which consider this point, two of the best are Glen St J. Barclay, *Friends in High Places: Australian–American Diplomatic Relations Since 1945*, Oxford University Press, Melbourne,1985; and TB Millar, 'From Whitlam to Fraser', *Foreign Affairs* vol. 55, no. 4, 1977, pp. 854–872. Millar observed that 'Labor's view of the world was … very different from that of its predecessors. … It believed there was value in having the United States available for some unforeseeable and remote crisis, but that in the meantime the United States would understandably accept a public kick in the shins from time to time to establish Australia's independent credentials' (p. 859). An interesting dissenting piece was by James Curran, 'Dear Mr President: How Whitlam Rattled the ANZUS Alliance', *The Monthly*, vol. 81, August 2012, www.themonthly.com.au/issue/2012/august/1348618116/james-curran/dear-mr-

governments viewed the US military involvement in Vietnam as fundamental to the defence of the Southeast Asian mainland; Australia contributed a modest Australian force component (up to 7,600 personnel at its peak strength and approximately 60,000 military personnel over the entire duration of that conflict) to support that campaign. By comparison, the US deployed nearly half a million military personnel to Vietnam in 1968 alone and over 2.7 million Americans served in the war.[23] As David McLean has since observed, '[w]ith American power seen as overwhelming, a policy by which the US would bear most of the risks of military intervention had enormous appeal to the Australian government, which sought to commit America to the region's defence at the lowest possible cost to Australia'.[24]

Bell noted that while dissent against the war grew among the 'articulate opinion-makers' (journalists, academics, students, parliamentarians, and intellectuals) during the mid-to-late 1960s, the wider sectors of the Australian electorate were still supportive of forward defence and military intervention in Southeast Asia.[25] This remained the case until the Americans themselves shifted away from confrontation and toward diplomacy following the January 1968 Tet Offensive, President Johnson's March 1968 resignation speech, and the announcement of the Guam Doctrine in August 1969. The growth of greater Australian independence within the alliance proved to be a gradual phenomenon because, Bell argued, Australian involvement in American wars have been largely diplomatic enterprises rather than military ones and have been predicated on the 'conventional wisdom' that American decision-making was naturally synonymous with Australia's national interests.[26] This presumption was, of course, tested during Whitlam's three-year term of office. However, it was the relatively chaotic way such adjustments were introduced—with an emphasis on declaratory style over relatively steady operational foreign policy management—that made the challenge to alliance orthodoxy appear much more radical than it really was.[27] Indeed, as Bell noted, key bilateral arrangements such as Washington's control over operations at intelligence installations in Australia were largely unchanged. Others, such as relations between the Australian and

---

president (accessed 2 September 2013). President Richard Nixon and his Secretary of State, Henry Kissinger, diplomatically isolated Australia for months after receiving a letter from Whitlam threatening to make his government's dissent to the US bombing of North Vietnam public. Also see David Martin Jones and Mike Lawrence Smith, 'Misreading Menzies and Whitlam: Reassessing the Ideological Construction of Australian Foreign Policy', *The Round Table*, vol. 89, no. 355, 2000, pp. 387–406.

23   David McLean, 'From British Colony to American Satellite? Australia and the USA During the Cold War', *Australian Journal of Politics and History*, vol. 52, no. 1, 2006, pp. 64–79, at 77; and David L Anderson, 'Vietnam War (1960–1975): Military and Diplomatic Course', in John Whiteclay Chambers (ed), *The Oxford Companion to Military History*, Oxford University Press, New York, 1999, pp. 759–763.

24   McLean, 'From British Colony to American Satellite?' p. 77.

25   Bell, *Dependent Ally*, pp. 77, 93–94.

26   ibid., p. 182.

27   ibid., p. 113.

American intelligence communities, were finessed at the public service level as first Nixon and later Whitlam became engrossed in their respective domestic political problems.[28]

Another key analysis in Bell's work on post-war alliance systems related to how effective they have been within the regional and global power balances within which they operate. She acknowledged that the North Atlantic Treaty Organization (NATO) was generally useful and effective in containing Soviet power during the Cold War.[29] She argued, however, that 'force goals' of NATO such as credible defence burden-sharing, and the eventual development of a strong and quasi-independent European military component, were never quite realised—this was largely because American power 'more than compensated for the local deficiencies' of NATO Europe. She posited that under the rubric of 'containment strategy', both NATO and the United States' Asia-Pacific alliances were actually an effective balance of power coalition with forward defence lines.[30]

Bell became increasingly critical of NATO once global bipolarity had been relegated to history and a multipolar global power balance was beginning to emerge. US power, she argued, was sufficient to manage Cold War bipolarity (1945–91), but had failed to come to terms with the global redistribution of power that had evolved after the Soviet Union's demise. She began promoting what many would view as radical ideas for alliance reform. Amongst the most prominent of these was to admit Russia as a full member of NATO. By doing so, the West could avoid Russia's marginalisation from the rest of Europe. Such an initiative, Bell insisted, would also infuse a sense of European identity that had been largely abandoned after the Cold War.[31] Indeed, NATO Europe had been exposed to a substantial dose of American nationalism during Ronald Reagan's presidency (1981–88) when Washington's then predominant neoconservative policy-makers regarded Europe as highly susceptible to 'Finlandisation'— overly subservient to intimidation by Soviet military power and too enamoured by the lure of détente.[32]

---

28 ibid., pp. 130–131.

29 When writing about European security in the late 1970s, Bell acknowledged that '[t]he survival of a military alliance for almost thirty years undoubtedly indicates that it is felt by the governments concerned to confer benefits. … On the whole the NATO relationship has been a comfortable enough one for the policy-makers concerned'. Coral Bell, *The Diplomacy of Détente: The Kissinger Era*, Martin Robertson, London, 1977, p. 99.

30 Coral Bell, *The Asian Balance of Power: A Comparison with European Precedents*, Adelphi Paper no. 44, International Institute for Strategic Studies, London, February 1968, p. 4.

31 Coral Bell, 'Why an Expanded NATO Must Include Russia', *Journal of Strategic Studies*, vol. 17, no. 4, 1994, pp. 27–41.

32 Coral Bell, 'The Reagan Administration and the American Alliance-Structure', *Australian Outlook*, vol. 41, no. 3, 1987, pp. 151–5.

Alliances and Concert Politics

The 11 September 2001 terrorist attacks in New York and Washington, DC, signalled that a global redistribution of power was under way that would render Washington's task of leading its alliances ever more difficult. Acknowledging that the 'Jihadist' challenge had introduced new factors of asymmetrical warfare into the calculations of US policy planners, Bell concluded in a widely acclaimed strategy paper written for the Australian Strategic Policy Institute, *Living with Giants,* that Washington's responses to this new type of non state-centric threat 'will put more strain on its alliances, both in the Atlantic and the Pacific, and further reduce US ability to induce "bandwagoning" by other powers'.[33] New forms of alignment would be required in a world increasingly shaped by complex multipolarity as the diffusion of American power intensified, especially following the ineffectual US invasion and occupation of Iraq. As she observed, '[p]ower is being redistributed all the time because of economic, demographic and technological changes beyond the control of even the most Machiavellian policy maker in Washington'.[34]

Bell suggested two new pathways to order-building: the strengthening of regional and international security communities, and the formation of great power concerts. She viewed these two approaches as symbiotic and working in ways that would render other models such as Samuel Huntington's 'clash of civilizations', Mearsheimer's 'hegemonic war', or even more remote variants such as 'Leagues of Democracies' and 'Anglospheres' less relevant in the twenty-first century.[35] Regional and international security communities would provide space for middle and small powers to promote their own interests and to cultivate common norms in something other than the tightly woven asymmetrical framework which intermittently frustrated Australia and other US allies during the Cold War. Bell cited the Asia-Pacific Economic Cooperation (APEC) grouping or an expanded Association of Southeast Asian Nations (ASEAN; the East Asia Summit emerged after Bell wrote this study although she predicted the forming of such an organisation) in the Asia-Pacific as illustrative typologies of regional community-building and potentially commensurate to the European Community and NATO that still appeared viable at the time of her writing. She theorised that the G8 and the burgeoning G20 economic groupings and other such arrangements could only expand and survive under an overarching framework

---

33   Coral Bell, *Living with Giants: Finding Australia's Place in a More Complex World,* Strategy Report, Australian Strategic Policy Institute, Canberra, April 2005, p. 14.

34   ibid., p. 31.

35   Samuel P. Huntington, *The Clash of Civilizations and the Remaking of World Order*, Simon & Schuster, New York, 1996; John J Mearsheimer, *The Tragedy of Great Power Politics*, Norton, New York, 2001; Ivo Daalder and James Lindsay, 'Democracies of the World, Unite', *The American Interest*, vol. 2, no. 3, 2007, pp. 5–15; and James C. Bennett, *The Anglosphere Challenge: Why the English-Speaking Nations Will Lead the Way in the Twenty-First Century*, Rowman & Littlefield, Lanham, 2007.

managed by the world's five great powers—China, the European Union, India, Japan, Russia, and the United States—acting in concert to regulate and enforce systemic rules based on their collective interests, curbing defections from this framework, and constantly negotiating adjustments to such an architecture to preserve global stability.

The key precondition for realising this construct would be to prevent the return to classic power balancing and particularly to avoid the emergence of any anti-hegemonic alliance directed toward the United States. A new Sino–Russian arrangement directed toward checking American power would be illustrative of resurgent power balancing undermining global stability. Bell recognised that convincing the United States to enter into such a system would be the greatest barrier to its realisation. However, the logic of her proposed framework was so compelling from her perspective that she readily endorsed its creation. Citing the prospect of nuclear weapons states in the Asia-Pacific miscalculating each others' intentions in future crises and thereby precipitating major wars no one wanted, she insisted that 'every middle or minor power in the region ought to be interested in a security community' nurtured by great power support. While not anticipating the global financial crisis which exploded on the scene five years after *Living with Giants* was published, she nevertheless anticipated US problems in holding the global economic and geopolitical orders together and recommended that Washington willingly relinquish its post-Cold War primacy: '[a]ll that Washington has to do to reconcile its fellow giants of the central balance … is to administer a unipolar world *as if it were* a concert of powers, and it will become one'.[36] In such a world, moreover, she believed that Australia could play a role in adjudicating American reconciliation of its post-war bilateral alliance system with Asia-Pacific institution-building similar to 'that Britain has long played in relations between the US and continental Europe'.[37]

Bell expanded on this thinking in what would be one of her last major pieces of work—a paper written for the Lowy Institute for International Policy entitled *The End of the Vasco da Gama Era*.[38] The voyages of 'that great [Portuguese] navigator' and his success in discovering a maritime trading route from Europe to India at the end of the fifteenth century symbolised the beginning of the West's commercial and strategic dominance which endured over the next five centuries. The beginning of the twenty-first century marks the rise of three great non-Western civilisations: Indian, Chinese, and Islamic. It also signals the

---

36   Bell, *Living with Giants*, pp. 27, 41; emphasis in original.
37   ibid., p. 54.
38   Coral Bell, *The End of the Vasco da Gama Era: The Next Landscape of World Politics,* Lowy Institute Paper 21, Lowy Institute for International Policy, Sydney, 2007. Much of the thinking for this work emanated from Bell's earlier work, *A World Out of Balance: American Ascendancy and International Politics in the 21st Century,* Longueville Books, Double Bay, 2003.

beginning of the end of the nation-state's monopoly on power distribution as non-state actors begin to play a more fundamental role in meeting a growing and diverse array of non-traditional security challenges.

How would classical alliance politics fare in such a dynamically shifting environment? Bell was somewhat ambiguous on this point. As was argued in *Living with Giants*, a major precondition for successful concert politics is to preclude the formation of an anti-hegemonic alliance against one of the great powers by ensuring (via negotiation or coercion) that none of them would pursue global hegemony. In developing this pre-condition, Bell largely concurred with Mearsheimer's view that hegemonic competition—complete with the alliance politics that would accompany it—would likely lead to general war. Unlike Mearsheimer, she did not regard such competition to be an inevitable feature of world politics if a viable great power concert materialised. Yet Bell acknowledged that using alliances to balance against threats remained a necessary policy component in certain circumstances, at least over the short-term. Japan's post-Cold War environment, for example, mandated a continued need for the US–Japan bilateral security alliance in the face of Chinese military modernisation and North Korean development of nuclear weapons.[39] British resistance to a truly autonomous European security community operating independently from NATO was equally unlikely to dissipate any time soon, and Bell noted that such a community could only materialise if Russia joined or closely aligned with it. Odds of a stronger and more independent Europe emerging to facilitate a global concert were also undermined by that continent's growing sense of vulnerability to Islamic power and a 'Muslim diaspora' growing within its boundaries.[40] Writing in 2007, Bell could not have anticipated the global financial crisis wreaking such a degree of financial havoc in Europe, but this event seriously undermined the idea of a Europe acting as a unified great power, either autonomously or in concert with other global power centres. Nor could she have anticipated the Barack Obama administration's endorsement of a 'pivot' or 'rebalancing' strategy for the Asia-Pacific in 2011 that is designed to reinforce the US bilateral alliance system in that region. Hence, her speculation that the 'hub and spokes' logic of post-war balancing in Asia may give way to a NATO-like multilateral framework more able to co-exist with a Sino–American deal to share power seems premature.[41] Indeed, Bell could never quite let go her conviction that at the end of the day, Australia remains inextricably and beneficially tied to US power as the best means for ensuring its own national security and for pursuing global stability:

---

39 Bell, *The End of the Vasco da Gama Era*, p. 23.
40 ibid., p. 28.
41 ibid., pp. 50–1. For definitive statements on the pivot strategy see Hillary Clinton, 'America's Pacific Century', *Foreign Policy*, vol. 189, November 2011, pp. 56–63; and Barack Obama, 'Remarks by President Obama to the Australian Parliament', Parliament House, Canberra, 17 November 2011, www.whitehouse.gov/the-press-office/2011/11/17/remarks-president-obama-australian-parliament (accessed 3 September 2013).

As middle powers go, Australia is exceptionally well endowed with both economic and strategic assets: remote location, a defensible sea-air gap, good access to intelligence, an alliance with the paramount power and efficient, well trained and well equipped forces. ... The United States will remain the paramount power of the society of states, only in a multipolar world instead of a unipolar or bipolar one.[42]

Conclusion

Coral Bell's major and continuing contribution to international security relations is the provision of nuanced and enduring judgements on how power balancing and the alliance politics that emanates from it relate to regional and global order-building. Her application of classical realism and historical analysis to explain why states coalesce to realise acceptable power equilibriums transcends the more abstract analysis represented by the second wave of alliance literature generated during the height of the Cold War. She did not view such behaviour (power balancing and alliance politics) as sufficiently mechanistic or repetitive to justifying surrendering to either the anarchical or systemic schools of thought that dominated academic thinking on alliances during that period. Interpreting history as the delicate art form that it is, and drawing up sophisticated portraits of how events unfolded the way they did, is seminal in understanding the security relations between those states and polities which matter the most to international stability. Bell never lost sight of this prerequisite when constructing her magisterial narratives of modern alliance politics.

As Hugh White has recently reminded us, Bell's willingness to follow where an argument leads and her openness to new ideas were her distinct trademarks. She complemented these traits, however, with a steady and profound sense of optimism about the future of world order.[43] This separates her from most other classical realists who too often limited their analyses to what they saw as the inevitabilities of strategic competition and war and neo-realists who surrendered to the all too easy temptation of viewing global structural changes as nothing more than a state's preordained and mechanistic process of survival through balancing to gain power and wealth at each others' expense.

Near the end of her life, Bell envisioned that the West could shape a complicated but practical hybrid approach to realising global stability, combining community-building and power-sharing in ways that would make the world

---

42   Bell, *The End of the Vasco da Gama Era*, p. 53.
43   Hugh White, 'Vote of Thanks to Kim Beazley', Coral Bell Lecture, Lowy Institute for International Policy, 19 March 2008, www.lowyinstitute.org/files/pubfiles/Beazley,_Thinking_security,_Vote_of_thanks.pdf (accessed 3 September 2013).

and those inhabiting it more secure. She sensed that she could contribute to our understanding of how more effective order-building could be realised at a time when the post-Cold War world was undergoing immense structural change. This spurred her on to refine her already formidable arguments about alliances, concerts, and community-building, and to engage with both key policy-makers and with her valued colleagues in academic and think-tank settings. No policy practitioner or independent analyst could aspire to do more.

13. Coral Bell and the Concert of Power: Avoiding Armageddon

Hugh White[1]

Coral Bell gave the title 'A Preoccupation with Armageddon' to the fragment of memoir found among her papers, and began it by recalling the moment she heard that the atom bomb had been dropped on Hiroshima. 'I can even remember the pattern of the hearth-rug on which I was standing when a colleague rushed in with the news', she wrote. 'Perhaps that moment is the reason why so much of my life has revolved around wars and crises; why I have had such a preoccupation with the possibility of Armageddon. Especially how to avoid it'.[2]

It is perfectly characteristic of Coral that this short and simple statement should so fully and precisely describe her life's work. Coral Bell was one of the very last of those whose thinking about international relations was shaped by direct and personal experience of hegemonic war, and her life's work was to explore the question about how such wars can be avoided. She looked for answers in the ways states interact with one another, both in the slowly-shifting patterns of their long-term relationships, and in sudden stresses of crisis. She believed the key to preserving peace was to be found in the nature and workings of the international system—the way states communicate with one another, understand one another, and reach and honour agreements with one another, and she devoted her long life and her formidable talents to studying the nature of those communications, understandings and agreements.

She explored how states could reach understandings and agreements which would forestall conflict, and as time passed she became convinced that one model of international understanding offered the best hope for doing that: the concert of power as exemplified by the European order of the century following the Congress of Vienna in 1815. In this essay I will try to trace the evolution of this conviction in her work, relate it to other ideas she developed, and explore her hopes that a concert of power would indeed prove to be the key to avoiding Armageddon in the twenty-first century. But we should start back on that hearth-rug on 6 August 1945.

---

1   I would like to thank especially my old friends and colleagues, Robert Ayson and Brendan Taylor, for stimulating discussions about the issues covered here.
2   Coral Bell 'A Preoccupation with Armageddon', unpublished memoir, Canberra, 2012, p. 1.

Preoccupation with Armageddon

We can picture Coral at that moment: a young woman of twenty-two, serious, shy but confident of her formidable intellect and perhaps also of her charm, quietly but profoundly determined to have a part in shaping the new world that would follow the war, and absolutely sure that avoiding another such war—especially, after Hiroshima, a nuclear war—was more important and more urgent than anything else. She never lost that conviction; never for a moment doubted that contributing to this great task was the whole point of working in the field of international relations, whether as a practitioner or a scholar. She left government for scholarship because she decided that she could contribute more that way, but as a scholar she remained always and absolutely engaged in practical questions of policy. She was never interested in the construction of theories for their own sake, and probably thought that colleagues who found theory more interesting than contemporary questions of policy lacked seriousness, and imagination. Her vivid sense that major war was not just a theoretical possibility but an ever-present danger, and her ability to imagine what such a war would be like and what it would mean, were the mainsprings of her work.

This made her a 'realist' in a specific and significant sense, though one far removed from the academic realism of people like Morgenthau. Hers was the realism of Machiavelli, whose cardinal insight, as Isaiah Berlin explained, was the incompatibility of our most treasured values—'that ends, equally sacred, may contradict one another'.[3] Although she was not much given to philosophising at this level of abstraction, Coral clearly understood and accepted this reality. Throughout her work it is clear that she sees that choices have to be made between the preservation of peace and other highly desirable objectives, and she was never in much doubt that peace should take priority. It would not be true to say that Coral believed in peace at any price, but she certainly believed that only something of truly exceptional value was worth a major war.

But unlike most realists Coral was also an optimist. She consistently and perhaps increasingly as time passed believed not just that states could reach and sustain agreements which minimised the risk of major war. She shared the English School's recognition that order and peace could be achieved despite the anarchy of international politics by understandings and cooperation between states. Such agreements were the key to avoiding Armageddon, and hence the perennial focus of her work, and later in her career she saw a concert of power as the most promising form for such agreements to take. Moreover towards the

---

3   Isaiah Berlin 'The Question of Machiavelli' *New York Review of Books,* 4 November 1971. www.nybooks. com/50/Machiavelli (accessed 6 August 2013).

end of her life she became increasingly convinced that an international order based on a 'concert of power' was in fact taking shape. But we have to go back much farther to see the beginnings of her thinking about it.

London

Coral had an excellent education in history, and there can be little doubt that she knew a good deal about the Concert of Europe well before she began her career as a scholar when she arrived in London in 1951. Over the following years she came to know and be influenced by a remarkable group which included Martin Wight, Hedley Bull and Alistair Buchan, whose approach to the study of international relations was, like Coral's, strongly based on the careful application of historical analogues to current questions. This group were certainly interested in the idea of a 'concert of power', and they referred to it quite often, though not at much length or in much detail. Coral herself seems (from my reading) not to have taken much interest in the 'concert of power' idea herself at this stage, but it seems fair to assume that this is where here ideas about it first evolved.

Coral's London colleagues were certainly struck by the fact that for a century after 1815 there was no hegemonic war between the great powers of Europe— that is, no war to establish, or prevent the establishment of, hegemony by any one power. So while there were serious wars in Europe over this time, none approached the catastrophic scale of the Revolutionary and Napoleonic wars that preceded it, or the World Wars that followed it. They believed that Europe avoided hegemonic war because of the nature of the relationships between the great powers themselves, which constituted a distinctive kind of international order. Two things made that order distinctive. One was a matter of style: the *way* they dealt with one another. As Martin Wight put it: 'the diplomatic system of the Concert maintained standards of good faith, mutual consideration and restraint higher perhaps than at any other time in international history'.[4]

The other was a matter of substance: the great power's objectives in dealing with one another. Hedley Bull saw the Concert of Power as an agreement among great powers 'that the maintenance of a general balance of power is a common objective',[5] while Herbert Butterfield wrote, 'The Concert of Europe was in

4   Martin Wight, 'Why is There No International Theory?', in Martin Wight and Herbert Butterfield (eds), *Diplomatic Investigations,* George, Allen & Unwin, London, 1966, p. 30.
5   Hedley Bull, *The Anarchical Society: A Study of World Politics,* Macmillan, London, 1979 p. 114. Bull offers a much wider definition later in *The Anarchical Society* (p. 225), where he writes of a concert as an agreement between great powers 'to join forces in promoting common policies throughout the international system as a whole.' His purpose here seems to be to distinguish the agreement underlying a concert from an agreement to divide the system into separate spheres of influence. This seems mistaken: there is no reason why a Concert in the narrower and more useful sense could not be based on a mutually accepted division into spheres of influence.

origin and essence a common agreement on the principle of the balance of power'.[6] Of course these descriptions lead to questions about the notoriously slippery concept of the 'balance of power' itself, but it is clear that both writers meant in these contexts that the essence of the 'concert of power' was an agreement among the great powers that none of them would try to upset the balance of power by seeking hegemony for themselves. One can also see that there is a close connection between the style and substance of great-power diplomacy under a concert, because the 'high standards', especially of restraint, that Wight mentioned were clearly essential to sustain the mutual forbearance about seeking hegemony that the concert entailed.

These scholars—especially Wight—did not necessarily see the 'concert of power' as a good thing. Wight doubted that it contributed much to the peace of Europe, which he believed owed more to the opportunities for expansion for the great powers outside Europe,[7] and likened the 'concert' to the later appeasement of fascism, which he said was, 'in a sense a continuation of the old system of the Concert of Europe whereby the great powers settled matters by private bargains among themselves at the expense of small powers'.[8]

Kissinger

The second big influence on Coral's thinking about the 'concert of power' idea seems to have been Henry Kissinger. The first time Coral seems to have focused directly on the concert of power was in her 1977 book *The Diplomacy of Détente: The Kissinger Era*, which as the title suggests was very much a study of Kissinger's approach to the diplomacy of order-building. Kissinger had of course begun his career with *A World Restored* about the Congress of Vienna at which the Concert of Europe was created, and the 'concert' idea remained central to his thinking.[9] The first point to note is that Kissinger's views of the 'concert of power' model were more positive than those of Coral's London colleagues. She wrote of the way Kissinger's policy of détente 'crystallises within itself the central moral tension not only of international politics but of politics in general: the tension between order and justice'. And she quotes approvingly

---

6   Herbert Butterfield, 'The Balance of Power', *Diplomatic Investigations*, p. 154.
7   Martin Wight, *Power Politics*, Royal Institutue of International Affairs, London, 1978, p. 42. The opposite could just as easily be true: the great powers were free to expand around the globe because they were secure from hegemonic challenges in Europe.
8   ibid., p. 214. Bull was also alive to the risks of great-power collusion at the expense of smaller powers, especially in the Cold War context between the US and the USSR. See *The Anarchical Society*, p. 297.
9   See Henry Kissinger, *A World Restored: Metternich, Castlereagh and the Problems of Peace , 1812-22*, Houghton Mifflin, Boston, 1973.

of Kissinger's resolution of this tension in favour of order, 'The preservation of human life and human society are moral values too'—and for Coral, as for Kissinger, this is what is at stake in avoiding Armageddon.[10]

In exploring the link between Kissinger's academic work and his policy practice Coral offered a very neat account of the 'concert' idea and its relationship to the concepts of balance of power and detente. It deserves to be quoted at some length:

> A World Restored is often described as being about the balance of power, but in fact it is about the working of *a concert of powers*. The distinction between the two is important for an understanding of its relevance to détente. Obviously a balance of power underlay the nineteenth-century concert of powers, or it would not have proved viable, just as a balance of power is now necessary as a foundation of détente, which is not yet a concert of powers. As Castlereagh once said, in a concert system the powers feel a common duty as well as a common interest. A balance of power may be regarded [as] a sort of force of history that tends to assert itself almost automatically in any system of independent sovereignties. A concert of power, on the other hand, must always be a construction of conscious statecraft.[11]

This passage brings out two key aspects of the 'concert of power' idea. First, there is the central question of the relationship between a concert of powers and a balance of power. A balance of power is necessary but not sufficient for a concert. One cannot build a concert unless there is already a balance of power, but much more than that is needed to create a concert. A balance of power system emerges quite spontaneously from the independent calculations of individual states about the best way to preserve their autonomy, but it does not prevent hegemonic war. As Hedley Bull wrote, the balance of power is not a system to prevent war, but to preserve the system of states from hegemony, if necessary though the use of war.[12] Thus a balance of power system was what remained when the Concert of Europe collapsed in 1914, and the European wars of the twentieth century—including the Cold War—were classic examples of a balance of power system at work to prevent hegemony through war. The point

---

10   Coral Bell, *The Diplomacy of Détente: The Kissinger Era*, St. Martin's Press, New York, 1977, pp. 32–33. There is a fascinating and important question here about the role of values in shaping and sustaining a concert of power. Must a concert be based on shared values? Indeed there are two questions; first, is it possible to build a concert without shared values? Second, is it right to do so? Castlereagh seems to suggest that a convergence of values is essential to a concert when he says that they are based on obligations not interests, and Hedley Bull in *The Anarchical Society* seems to argue that at least a measure of justice is required for a concert to work. I'm not so sure. See Robert Ayson, 'Is Minimal Order Enough?', Hugh White, 'Strategic Parsimony', and Hugh White, 'Response to Commentary on *The China Choice*', in *Security Challenges*, vol. 9, no. 1, 2013.
11   Bell, *The Diplomacy of Détente*, p. 25.
12   Bull, *The Anarchical Society*, p. 107.

of a concert is to avoid hegemony without the need for such wars. To do that the balance of power must be maintained not by war but by agreement. This is why a concert 'must always be a construction of conscious statecraft'.

Second, there is the question of what is required to construct the agreements which convert a balance of power into a concert of power. The view attributed to Castlereagh in the passage quoted above suggests that it requires more than simply a shared interest in the prevention of war, but mutual acceptance of higher obligation going beyond that interest. The same idea is hinted at in the idea that the essence of a concert is a higher sense of good faith and obligation as expressed in the quote from Wight above. I'm not sure it's right, and in the end I don't think Coral did either. For her, and for me, the key difference in this respect between a balance of power and a concert of power is not that one is based on interest and the other on obligation, but the nature of the interest being served. The difference is that in a balance of power system the key interest being served for each party is to preserve its independence by avoiding hegemony, whereas in a concert of power each party is also driven by an interest in avoiding war at the same time. To so this they are willing to forgo any chance of achieving hegemony themselves, and undertake instead to respect the independence of all the other parties. A viable concert of power depends on the strength of that undertaking and its credibility with the other parties. The key to creating and sustaining a concert of power is to understand how these undertakings can be created and made credible.

Cold War — Negotiating from Strength

These insights take us back to some of Coral's much earlier work, where we can see her intense interest in issues which are essential to the idea of a concert, long before she saw them specifically in that context. Her first monograph, *Negotiation from Strength: A Study in the Politics of Power*,[13] which was published in 1963, explores an idea that was prevalent in America throughout the 1950s. It was that the US should defer any serious negotiation on accommodation with the Soviet Union until its military position had improved to the point that it would be able to avoid making any substantial concessions to the Soviets in return for a reduction in tensions. Coral says that this is mistaken because US strength did not in fact increase relative to the Soviets over the 1950s, and also, more fundamentally, because America's overriding interests in avoiding war with the Soviets justified substantial concessions to reach an accommodation. The whole book thus focuses on the circumstances under which the US and Soviets might

---

13   Coral Bell, *Negotiation from Strength: A Study in the Politics of Power*, Chatto & Windus, London, 1962, and Alfred A. Knopf, New York, 1963.

be willing to make the kind of accommodation required to reach a concert-like understanding with one another that would avoid the risk of war, and the imperative to do so.

Only a year or two later Coral saw signs of a more hopeful attitude emerging on both sides of the Cold War divide. In 1964 she wrote of the emergence between the US and the USSR of what she called a 'shadow condominium', the basic function of which is 'their joint management of the central power balance'.[14] Coral saw this as essentially a crisis-management mechanism in which the central powers acted together to ensure that peace between them was maintained, if necessary at the expense of the interests if smaller powers, and she cited the Cuban Missile Crisis as an early example of the shadow condominium in action. Brendan Taylor is surely correct in seeing in this concept the seeds of a 'concert of power' idea, albeit one that incorporates a great deal of competition along with occasional bouts of cooperation.[15] What is common between a concert of power and Coral's shadow condominium is the willingness of both powers to sacrifice key interests in order to avoid war with one another. The difference is that in the shadow condominium this willingness only comes into play in times of crisis, whereas in a concert (or one might say, a condominium pure and simple) this willingness frames the management of relationships more or less continually. But it is striking that Coral saw signs of such willingness in 1964.[16]

In the years that followed those signs became much clearer, as the US and USSR moved towards the kinds of mutual understandings that many believed at the time heralded the end of the Cold War. Coral's intense interest in this process was shown in her book on détente in which, as we have seen, she looked very closely at the idea of a 'concert of power'. She was clear that détente did not itself constitute a 'concert' system, but she clearly saw that as one direction in which it might evolve and the image she sketched of that possibility in this book strikingly resembled her ideas of a post Cold War concert of power which emerged in the 1990s. She wrote that an optimistic view of US–Soviet détente in the 1970s could see it as 'a mode of attempting to transmute "a revolutionary order" (which the twentieth century clearly has been and remains) into a "legitimate order" by spinning a sort of web of common interests and arrangements between the revolutionary and status quo powers'.[17] This, she implied, would be a kind of 'concert', but she cautioned that this was not to assume that such an order would be possible in the late twentieth century. She

---

14   Coral Bell, *The Debatable Alliance: An Essay in Anglo-American Relations,* Chatham House Essays No. 3, Oxford University Press, London, 1964, p. 111.

15   Brendan Taylor 'A US-China "Shadow Condominium"?' *The Strategist,* Australian Strategic Policy Institute, 25 October 2012. http://www.aspistrategist.org.au/a-us-china-shadow-condominium/ (accessed 6 August 2013).

16   Others did too, as Robert Ayson has pointed out to me, including Thomas Schelling and Hedley Bull, who saw the Test Ban Treaty of 1963 as evidence for this kind of cooperation.

17   Bell, *The Diplomacy of Détente,* p. 26.

quoted Kissinger explaining that many things that made a concert of power possible in the nineteenth Century were not available in the twentieth. 'The stable technology, the multiplicity of great powers, the limited domestic claims and the frontiers which permitted adjustment have gone forever.'[18] That's a fascinating list of the conditions required for a concert of power, but it may be too demanding, and not all of the conditions turned out to be 'gone forever'. Interestingly for the way Coral's thinking about the concert of power model evolved later, she emphasised that 'any viable concert of power would ... have to be in a world basis'. In a preceding passage she wrote:

> Any workable concert system for the late twentieth century, as against the early nineteenth, would have to include some non-European members. One can perhaps see emerging in contemporary international relations what might be called the candidate-members of some prospective world concert of powers, in countries like Brazil or Nigeria or Iran.[19]

Coral dismissed all this as too optimistic for serious policy-making, and maintained her primary focus on the less ambitious and more urgent aim of using détente to make the Cold War safer. But this did not stop her setting down an eerily prescient sketch of how the conditions for her model of a global concert might evolve:

> A really optimistic American view of Cold War would presumably hold that the Soviet Union could somehow be made to shrink as a power, allowing Eastern Europe to regain its autonomy and ending any serious military threat and any possibility of the expansion of Soviet influence overseas. But this is a very unrealistic expectation.[20]

After the Cold War

It is hardly surprising then that when this 'very unrealistic expectation' did nonetheless come to pass, Coral immediately began to argue that the form of international order most likely to replace the bipolar balance of the Cold War was a concert of power. She presented this case first in a short monograph, *The Post-Soviet World: Geopolitics and Crises,* published in 1992, in which she argued that 'the emerging (or re-emerging) pattern of great power relationships

18   ibid., p. 27.
19   ibid., p. 26.
20   ibid., p. 27.

is that of a concert of powers, somewhat akin to that after 1815, though of course global rather than merely European, and based on six great powers rather than five'.[21]

Coral had two reasons for thinking that a concert of powers was emerging at this time. The first was her belief—widely shared at the time—that with the end of the Cold War the US–Soviet bipolarity had given way to a multipolar distribution of power in which a number of great powers would all play more or less functionally equal roles. This was of course necessary for the emergence of a concert of power, but it was not sufficient, because a reversion to multipolarity might have produced only reversion to a classic balance of power system.[22] Her second reason for thinking that a concert of power was then emerging was that she saw evidence that the understandings between great powers necessary for a concert of power were indeed emerging as bipolarity gave way to multipolarity. For this evidence she looked primarily to the functioning of the UN Security Council in the early 1990s, and especially the way the great powers behaved in the Gulf crisis of 1990–91 following Iraq's invasion of Kuwait. The fact that the Security Council had begun to work as originally intended showed, she argued, that the concert of power which had underlain its original design had been revived, albeit with a different membership from that embodied in the Council itself.[23]

In developing this argument Coral gave an interesting account of the idea of a concert of power and how it differs from a balance of power, and the nature of the understandings which make the difference. She wrote:

> The difference between a workable concert of powers and an ordinary multilateral balance of power is that a concert system requires consciousness on the part of the central balance decision-makers that (at least for the time being) the common interests of their respective countries *vis a vis* the rest of the society of states are more important than their competitive interests *vis a vis* one another. That consciousness can only emerge when adversarial tensions between the central balance powers are at an unusually low ebb: that is, when the element of plausible challenge to the *status quo* of power distribution is either absent, as it is at the moment, or comes from outside the central balance.[24]

---

21   Coral Bell, *The Post-Soviet World: Geopolitics and Crises,* Canberra Papers on Strategy and Defence No.98, Strategic and Defence Studies Centre, The Australian National University, 1992, p. 2.

22   Coral had explored how a reversion to multipolarity in Asia would lead to a classic balance of power in an Adephi Paper published in 1968 in which she acknowledged no prospect of a concert emerging. See Coral Bell, *The Asian Balance of Power: A Comparison with European Precedents,* Adelphi Paper no. 44, International Institute for Strategic Studies, London, February 1968.

23   ibid., p. 6.

24   ibid., p. 4.

There are several notable things about this passage. The first is that it very clearly sees the concert as involving great powers (or 'central balance powers' as she also calls them) alone. She identifies six great powers in the post-Soviet world: America, Russia, Europe, China, Japan and India.[25] Second, when compared with the account in *The Diplomacy of Détente*, we can see a shift in Coral's thinking about what drives the great powers to form a concert. The earlier account focuses on the interests they share in avoiding war with one another, whereas this later account instead on the interests they share in managing their relations with, and responding to pressures and threats from, countries outside the group of great powers. Third, she expresses confidence that the adversarial tensions among the great powers are indeed 'at a low ebb', though she acknowledges in a later passage that this might not last, especially as economic relativities shift, though she saw this working more in Europe's favour than in, say, China's.[26] We will come back to each of these points as we explore how Coral's thinking about the 'concert of power' idea evolved in the last phase of her work.

After 9/11

Most people, including I think Coral herself, would agree that she had been premature in seeing the emergence of a concert in the early 1990s, because the first requirement for a concert—a bipolar or multipolar distribution of power—did not in fact eventuate. By the mid 1990s it had become commonplace to see the post-Cold War order not as multipolar but as unipolar, with the US emerging as the uncontested and incontestable leading power. Coral acknowledged this when she returned to exploring the future of the global order in 2005. In a paper for the Australian Strategic Policy Institute titled *Living with Giants: Finding Australia's Place in a More Complex World*[27] she acknowledged that America had become the leader in a unipolar global order, but then went on to explain why she thought this was coming to an end, to be replaced by a new multipolar order. 'There is thus, to my mind, an emerging prospect of the transmutation of the present unipolar society of states back into a multipolar one in the foreseeable future …', she wrote.[28] And not surprisingly she again predicted that this new multipolar order would function as a concert of powers.

---

25   ibid., pp. 4–5.
26   ibid., p. 5.
27   Coral Bell, *Living with Giants: Finding Australia's Place in a More Complex World*, Strategy Report, Australian Strategic Policy Institute, Canberra, April 2005.
28   ibid., p. 14.

Coral developed and elaborated this idea over the following years, most notably in one of her last major publications for the Lowy Institute called *The End of the Vasco da Gama Era: The Next Landscape of World Politics.*[29]

In these last works Coral saw two forces driving the global system from unipolarity to multipolarity. The less immediate of these, she believed, was the shift in the distribution of power itself, with the rise of a large number of powerful states including many from the developed world, to create what she called a 'company of giants'. Members of her company were characterised primarily by size, and especially size of population, which Coral seems to have considered at this point as more significant than economic weight.

> The emerging set of polities for the next central balance range from 'super-size' (China and India at more than a billion each), to those at several hundred million (the US at about 400 million, the EU at maybe 500 million or more, depending on recruitment), with Nigeria, Indonesia, Pakistan and Brazil in the next league. At the lower end of the scale, with a mere 100 million or so, are Russia, Japan, Mexico and others. This would mean a central balance of power, or alternatively a concert of powers, running to twelve or so members, rather like the eighteenth century.[30]

However Coral saw the primary factor driving the replacement of unipolarity by a multipolar order over the next decade or two was the collapse in the legitimacy of US leadership thanks to the mistakes of the Bush Administration in its conduct of the War on Terror. She argued that thanks to follies like the invasion of Iraq, America risked facing the kind of classic anti-hegemonic coalition that had so often merged against leading powers in the past. This, rather than the shift in relate economic weight, was what would prevent America maintaining leadership of a unipolar global order over the next few decades.[31] She correctly understood that unipolarity, while it lasted, always depended less on America's preponderance of power than on others' willingness to accept rather than contest US primacy.

Of course a simple anti-hegemonic coalition against the US would have produced a multipolar order functioning though a balance of power. Coral however argued that there was good reason to hope that we would see instead the emergence of a global concert of power among this large group of 'giants'. The factor that would drive them to form a concert rather than settle into a balance of power

29   Coral Bell, *The End of the Vasco da Gama Era: The Next Landscape of World Politics,* Lowy Institute Paper 21, Lowy Institute for International Policy, Sydney, 2007.
30   Bell, *Living with Giants,* p.29. In her later Lowy paper Coral seemed to step back from this expansive view of the membership of a concert, and limit it to six great powers with a wider group of nine or so major players outside it. See Bell, *The End of the Vasco da Gama Era,* p. 13.
31   ibid., p. 14.

system was the threat posed to all of them by what Coral called the 'Jihadist' threat to the global order.[32] This interesting idea harks back to Coral's views on the nature of concert of power systems which she set out in her discussion of détente thirty years before. Then, as we have seen, she suggested that a concert could be created by the need of the 'central powers' to respond to pressures from outside their group, rather than to restrain rivalry and avoid conflict with one another. The 'Jihadists' would seem to fit this model perfectly, because Coral believed they posed a threat to global order comparable to that posed by the First and Second World Wars and the Cold War.[33] She saw her 'company of giants' as united by a shared need to respond to this threat effectively, thus creating the conditions for a concert of power between them. Moreover she saw new forms and forums for global multilateral cooperation, like the G20, as both showing that the will existed among the great powers to create a concert, and as offering a path towards realising it.[34] Her hopes for the G20 were strengthened during the global financial crisis when its meetings were raised to leaders' level and it became, at least for a time, the premier global forum. The prospect that this enhanced G20 would become the basis for a global concert of power was the subject of one of her last, unpublished writings.[35]

There was obviously a lot of optimism in this analysis, but Coral was careful to point out that she was not assuming all would be easy between the great powers; she pointed out that things had hardly been rosy between Europe's great powers in the nineteenth century, and she explained at some length why it would be in each power's interests to support progress towards a concert.[36] She acknowledged moreover that the most difficult question among the great powers would be the management of relations between the US and China as China's economic and strategic weight grew. She was however optimistic that certain strong opposition would deter China from any hegemonic ambitions, even in its own backyards,[37] and that America was already well on the way to accommodating China's more modest ambitions for greater regional influence.[38] This made her hopeful that relations between them could remain manageable, and above all peaceful.

---

32 ibid., p. 20. In her later Lowy paper Coral said that climate change and the proliferation of nuclear weapons would also constitute challenges that would help unify the central powers and drive them to cooperate in a concert, though it seems clear that her main focus was on the 'Jihadist' threat. See Bell, *The End of the Vasco da Gama Era*, pp. 16–17.

33 ibid., p. 20, 40.

34 Bell, *The End of the Vasco da Gama Era*, p. 19.

35 Coral Bell, 'The G20 and Multipolarity', unpublished paper, Canberra, 2012.

36 Bell, *The End of the Vasco da Gama Era*, pp. 17–37.

37 ibid., p. 20.

38 ibid., pp. 33–4. Note there may be a certain tension here between Coral's confidence that China would not be allowed to establish local hegemony, and her assertion that America was already inclined to allow this.

Envoi

At the end of her long life, then, Coral remained focused on how the international system could best be managed to avoid Armageddon. It is hard not to be beguiled by the blend of determined optimism and hard reasoning which, from first to last, she brought to this task. But we must ask: how far was she right to see in the concert of power the best and perhaps only model for a stable, peaceful international order in the twenty-first century? I think she was much more right than wrong. I have argued elsewhere that a 'Concert of Asia' offers the best and perhaps only way to avoid escalating strategic rivalry between Asia's great powers over coming decades, for reasons which have much in common with Coral's and owe much to her analyses.[39] But there are two ways in which I'd differ from her analysis and predictions.

First, it seems to me that an effective concert must be smaller than Coral sometimes envisaged—only the great powers are involved[40]—and that it is much more likely to be a regional than a global arrangement, because the redistribution of wealth and power now underway is dismantling the global strategic system of recent centuries. Second, and more fundamentally, I think Coral was too optimistic about what would be required for a concert of power to evolve, and what the chances are of that happening. I do not think the 'Jihadist' threat—or the other unifying external challenges—has or will prove big enough to overshadow the tensions inherent between the region's major powers, and especially between the US and China.

That is, firstly, because I think the shift in relative economic and strategic weight between them is more fundamental and thus more disruptive to the established patterns of their relationship than Coral allows. By calling this shift 'the end of the Vasco da Gama era' Coral leaves us in no doubt that she sees how big this is. But even so her focus on demographics rather than economics does lead her to overlook just how much more important China's rise is to the redistribution of power than the other trends she mentions. This also leads her to underestimate the scale of the challenge it poses to the United States' power in Asia and its role in the Asian order. And secondly, this is because she overstates both the United States' and China's willingness to accommodate one another's very different expectations about their future relationships. For both countries these weigh far more in their thinking than the 'Jihadist' threat, or the global financial crisis, or anything else. They go to deep questions of national self-identity. Coral is absolutely right to see a mutual accommodation of these differences as entirely

---

39   Hugh White, *The China Choice: Why America Should Share Power*, Black Inc., Melbourne, 2012.
40   ibid., p. 141.

possible, and as offering a robust foundation for a stable concert of power system if it can be achieved. But she underestimated how hard it will be, and how likely is failure.

The challenge she has left us is to prove her optimism justified by seeing what can be done to improve the chances of building a concert of power in Asia. That means exploring what exactly would be required to achieve an accommodation between the US and China—and Asia's other great powers—that would provide the basis for peace. One might say that the best way to honour Coral's life and work is to throw ourselves into that task, because she was right: avoiding another hegemonic war—especially a nuclear war—remains more important and more urgent than anything else.

Appendix: Coral's Publications

Books

Survey of International Affairs for 1954, Oxford University Press, London, 1956.

Negotiation from Strength: A Study in the Politics of Power, Chatto & Windus, London, 1962, and Alfred A. Knopf, New York, 1963.

The Debatable Alliance: An Essay in Anglo-American Relations, Chatham House Essays No. 3, Oxford University Press, London, 1964.

The Conventions of Crisis: A Study in Diplomatic Management, Oxford University Press for the Royal Institute of International Affairs, London and New York, 1971.

The Diplomacy of Détente: The Kissinger Era, St. Martin's Press, New York, 1977; and Martin Robertson, London, 1977.

Dependent Ally: A Study in Australian Foreign Policy, Allen & Unwin, Sydney, 1984.

The Reagan Paradox: U.S. Foreign Policy in the 1980s, Rutgers University Press, New Brunswick, and Edward Elgar, Aldershot, 1989.

A World Out of Balance: American Ascendancy and International Politics in the 21st Century, Longueville Books, Double Bay, 2003.

Edited Books

Europe Without Britain, Cheshire, Melbourne, 1963.

Agenda for the Eighties: Contexts of Australian Choices in Foreign and Defence Policy, Australian National University Press, Canberra, 1980.

Agenda for the Nineties: Studies of the Contexts for Australian Choices in Foreign and Defence Policy, Longham Cheshire, Melbourne, 1991.

Nation, Region and Context: Studies in Peace and War in Honour of Professor T. B. Millar, Strategic and Defence Studies Centre, Canberra, 1995.

Co-editor (with Meredith Thatcher), *Remembering Hedley,* ANU E Press, 2008.

Monographs

The Asian Balance of Power: A Comparison with European Precedents, Adelphi Paper no. 44, International Institute for Strategic Studies, London, February 1968.

Crises and Australian Diplomacy, Arthur F Yencken Memorial Lecture 1972, Australian National University Press, Canberra, 1973.

President Carter and Foreign Policy: The Costs of Virtue?, Canberra Studies in World Affairs, The Australian National University, no. 1, 1980.

Academic Studies and International Politics: Papers of a Conference held at the Australian National University, June 1981, Canberra Studies in World Affairs, The Australian National University, no. 6, 1982.

Crises and Policy-Makers, Canberra Studies in World Affairs, The Australian National University, no. 10, 1982.

Communication Strategies: An Analysis of International Signalling Patterns, The Council for Arms Control, London, 1983.

Ethnic Minorities and Australia's Relations with the World, Canberra Studies in World Affairs, The Australian National University, no. 11, 1983.

Dependent Ally: A Study of Australia's Relations with the United States and the United Kingdom since the Fall of Singapore, Canberra Studies in World Affairs, The Australian National University, no. 15, 1984.

Forty Years On: Studies of World Change in the Four Decades (ed.), Canberra Studies in World Affairs, The Australian National University, no. 18, 1986.

Politics, Diplomacy and Islam: Four Case Studies, Canberra Studies in World Affairs, The Australian National University, no. 21, 1986.

The Unquiet Pacific, Centre for Security and Conflict Studies, London, 1987.

The Changing Pacific: Four Case Studies (ed.), Canberra Studies in World Affairs, The Australian National University, no. 22, 1987.

Australia's Alliance Options: Prospect and Retrospect in a World of Change, Australian Foreign Policy Publications Program, The Australian National University, Canberra, 1991.

The Post-Soviet World: Geopolitics and Crises, Canberra Papers on Strategy and Defence no. 98, Strategic and Defence Studies Centre, The Australian National University, 1992.

The United Nations and Crisis Management: Six Studies, Canberra Papers on Strategy and Defence no.104, Strategic and Defence Studies Centre, The Australian National University, 1994.

A Mixed Bag of Dilemmas: Australia's Policy-Making in a World of Changing International Rules, Research Paper no. 24, Department of the Parliamentary Library Information and Research Services, Canberra, 1999–2000.

'The Diplomatic Underpinnings of Security', in *Scoping Studies: New Thinking on Security* (ed.), Strategy Report, Australian Strategic Policy Institute, Canberra, 2004.

Living with Giants: Finding Australia's Place in a More Complex World, Strategy Report, Australian Strategic Policy Institute, Canberra, April, 2005.

The End of the Vasco da Gama Era: The Next Landscape of World Politics, Lowy Institute Paper 21, Lowy Institute for International Policy, Sydney, 2007.

Book Chapters

'The Diplomatic Meanings of "Europe"', in FW Cheshire (ed), *Europe without Britain: Six Studies of Britain's Application to Join the Common Market and its Breakdown*, Australian Institute of International Affairs, Melbourne, 1963.

'Australia and China: Power Balance and Policy', in AM Halpern (ed), *Policies Towards China: Views from Six Continents,* McGraw Hill, Sydney, 1965.

'The Containment of China', *The Yearbook of World Affairs Vol 22,* The London Institute of World Affairs and Steven and Sons, London, 1968.

'The Foreign Policy of China', in FS Northedge (ed), *The Foreign Policies of the Powers,* Praeger, New York, 1968.

'The Special Relationship', in M Leifer (ed), *Constraints and Adjustments in British Foreign Policy*, Allen & Unwin, Sydney, 1973.

'The Adverse Partnership', in C Holbraad (ed), *Superpowers and World Order,* Australian National University Press, Canberra, 1971.

'Australia in the Indian Ocean', in AJ Cottrell and RM Burrell (ed), *The Indian Ocean: Its Political, Economic, and Military Importance*, Praeger, New York, 1972.

'Security Preoccupations and Power Balances after Vietnam', in MW Zacher and RS Milne (ed), *Conflict and Stability in South-East Asia*, Anchor Press, New York, 1974.

'The Diplomacy of Deterrence', in HS Commager (ed), *The American Destiny: A Bicentennial History of the United States*, Orbis/Danbury Press, New York, 1976.

'Détente and American National Interest', in RN Rosencrance (ed), *America as an Ordinary Country: U.S. Foreign Policy and the Future*, Cornell University Press, Ithaca, 1976.

'Crisis Diplomacy', in L Martin (ed), *Strategic Thought in the Nuclear*, John Hopkins University Press, Washington, 1981.

'The Decline of Détente', in M Borstein (ed), *East-West Relations and the Future of Eastern Europe*, Allen & Unwin, Sydney, 1981.

'Crises and Survival', in *The Yearbook of World Affairs Vol 36*, The London Institute of World Affairs and Steven and Sons, London, 1982.

'The Case for the Alliance', in R O'Neill and D Horner (eds), *Australian Defence in the 1980s,* Strategic and Defence Studies Centre, Canberra, 1982.

'Australia in a World of Powers', in PJ Boyce and JR Angel (ed), *Independence and Alliance: Australia in World Affairs 1976-80*, Allen & Unwin, Sydney, 1983.

'Local Threats and the Central Balance', in *Academic Studies and International Politics*, Australian National University Press, Canberra, 1983.

'The Nexus between Economics, Politics & Strategy', in P Dibb (ed), *Australia's External Relations in the 1980s: The Interaction of Economic, Political and Strategic Factors*, Croom Helm Australia, Canberra, 1983.

'China and the International Order', *The Expansion of International Society*, in H Bull and A Watson (eds), Oxford University Press, Oxford, 1984.

'Crisis Analysis', in D Ball (ed), *Strategy and Defence: Australian Essays*, Allen & Unwin, Sydney, 1985.

'How Have We Survived the Crises?', in C Bell (ed), *Forty Years On: Studies of World Change in the Four Decades*, Canberra Studies in World Affairs, The Australian National University, No.18, 1986.

'ANZUS in Australia's Foreign and Security Policies', in J Bercovitch (ed), *ANZUS in Crisis: Alliance Management in International Affairs,* Macmillan, London, 1988.

'The International Environment and Australia's Foreign Policy', in F Mediansky and AC Palfreeman (eds), *In Pursuit of National Interests: Australian Foreign Policy in the 1990s,* Australian National University Press, Canberra, 1988.

'Journey with Alternative Maps', in J Kruzel and JN Rosenau (eds), *Journeys through World Politics: Autobiographical Reflections of Thirty-four Academic Travelers,* Lexington Books, Lexington, 1989, pp. 339–50.

'American Policy in the Third World', in Robert O'Neill and RJ Vincent, (eds), *The West and the Third World,* Macmillan, London, 1990, pp. 51–66.

'The International System and Changing Strategic Norms', in R Ayson and D Ball (eds), *Strategy and Security in the Asia-Pacific,* Allen & Unwin, Sydney, 2006.

Journal Articles

'The United Nations and the West', *International Affairs,* vol. 29, no. 4, October 1953, pp. 464–472.

'Korea and the Balance of Power', *Political Quarterly,* vol. 25, no. 1, January-March 1954, pp. 17–29.

'Britain in the Pacific', *Quarterly Review,* July 1954.

'American Leadership in the Western World', *India Quarterly,* vol. 17, no. 2, April 1965, pp. 150–161.

'President Kennedy and Foreign Policy', *Australian Quarterly,* vol. 34, no. 4, December 1962, pp. 7–21.

'Australia and the American Alliance', *The World Today,* vol. 19, no. 7, July 1963, pp. 302–310.

'Non-Alignment and the Power Balance', *Australian Outlook,* vol. 17, no. 2, August 1963, pp. 117–129.

'The Persistent Triangle', *International Journal,* vol. 19, no. 2, Winter 1964-65, pp. 219–223.

'The Diplomacy of Mr. Dulles', *International Journal,* vol. 20, no. 1, Winter, 1964-65, pp. 90–96.

'US–China Relations', *Current Affairs Bulletin,* April 1965.

'South–East Asia and the Powers', *The World Today,* vol. 21, no. 4, April 1965, pp. 137–150.

'The Architecture of Stability in South Asia', *The World Today,* vol. 22, no. 4, April 1966, pp. 151–160.

'Asian Crises and Australian Security', *The World Today,* vol. 23 no. 2, February 1967, pp. 80–88.

'The State of the Discipline: I.R.', *Quadrant,* vol. 12, no. 1, January-February 1968, pp. 79–84.

'Power and Anguish', *International Journal,* vol. 23, no. 3, Summer 1968, pp. 471–476.

'Strategic Problems of the Atlantic', *Moderne Welt,* no. 3/69, 1969.

'Security in Asia: Reappraisals after Vietnam', *International Journal,* vol. 24, no. 1, Winter 1968, pp. 1–12.

'Oedipal Politics', *Current Affairs Bulletin,* May 1969.

'The Adverse Partnership', *New Society,* January 1970.

'A Game of Jeopardy', *New Society,* June 1970.

'The Politics of Tribal Feeling', *New Society,* December 1970.

'Ireland: The Dynamics of Insurgency', *New Society,* November 1971.

'The Contest for Asia: A New Diplomacy', *New Society,* February 1972.

'A Case Study in Crisis Management During Détente', *International Affairs,* vol. 50, no. 4, October 1974, pp. 531–543.

'Kissinger in Retrospect: The Diplomacy of Power-Concert', *International Affairs,* vol. 53, no. 2, April 1977, pp. 202–216.

'Virtue Unrewarded: Carter's Foreign Policy at Mid-Term', *International Affairs,* vol. 54, no. 4, October 1978, pp. 559–572.

'Problems in Australian Foreign Policy', *Australian Journal of Politics and History,* vol. 24, no. 3, December 1978, pp. 292–300.

'Mr Fraser and Australian Foreign Policy', *The World Today,* vol. 35, no. 10, October 1979, pp. 414–420.

'The Prospects for Peace and War', *New Society,* November 1979.

'The United States and the Strategic Balance', *World Review,* October 1981.

'Superpower Perspectives on the Middle East: the View from Washington', *World Review,* August 1982.

'Hawke in Office: Towards Bipartisanship in Australian Foreign Policy', *TheWorld Today,* vol. 40, no. 2, February 1984, pp. 65–72.

'Decision-Makers and Crises', *International Journal,* vol. 39, no. 2, 1984, pp. 324–336.

'The Case Against Neutrality', *Current Affairs Bulletin,* September 1984.

'From Carter to Reagan', *Foreign Affairs,* vol. 63, no. 3, January 1985, pp. 490–510.

'Jeopardy and Survival', *The National Interest,* December 1985.

'The Goings and Comings of Détente', *Australian Outlook,* April 1986.

'The Reagan Administration and the American Alliance-Structure', *Australian Outlook*, vol. 41, no. 3, 1987, pp. 151–5.

'The American Establishment in Triumph and Fracture', *Quadrant,* vol. 32, no. 10, October 1988, pp. 14–17.

'Negotiation from Strength Revisited', *The National Interest,* no. 11, 1989.

'The Winning of the Cold War', *Quadrant,* vol. 34, no. 3, March 1990, pp. 13–24.

'The Future of Power in World Affairs', *Quadrant,* vol. 39, no. 9, September 1995, pp. 49–56.

'Why an Expanded NATO Must Include Russia', *Journal of Strategic Studies,* vol. 17, no. 4, 1994, pp. 27–41.

'A Hard and Bitter Peace: The Cold War in Retrospect', *Quadrant,* vol. 40, no. 3, March 1996, pp. 18–22.

'World Out of Balance?', *Quadrant,* vol. 41, no. 7–8, 1997, pp. 35–40.

'Washington and its Allies', *Quadrant,* vol.41, no. 1–2, 1997, pp. 19–24.

'American Ascendancy and the Pretense of Concert', *The National Interest,* no. 57, October 1999, p. 55.

'East Timor, Kosovo, Norms and Sovereignty', *Australian Quarterly,* vol. 72, no. 1, Feb-March 2000, pp. 12–15.

'East Timor, Canberra and Washington: A Case Study in Crisis Management', *Australian Journal of International Affairs,* vol. 54, no. 2, July 2000, pp. 171–176.

'Normative Shift', *The National Interest,* no. 70, Winter 2002/2003, pp. 44–54.

'Iraq, Alliances and Crisis Management', *Australian Journal of International Affairs,* vol. 57, no. 2, 2003, pp. 223–233.

'Exits from Wars', *The Sydney Papers*, vol. 16, no. 3, 2004.

'The Twilight of the Unipolar World', *The American Interest*, vol. 1, no. 2, Winter 2005, pp. 18–29.

'Seven Years to Get it Right', *American Review,* November 2009.

Working Papers

The Changing Central Balance and Australian Policy, Working Paper No. 1/1989, Department of International Relations, The Australian National University, August 1989.

The Cold War in Retrospect: Diplomacy, Strategy and Regional Impact, Working Paper No. 298, Strategic and Defence Studies Centre, The Australian National University, Canberra, 1996.

The First War of the 21st Century: Asymmetric Hostilities and the Norms of Conduct, Working Paper No. 364, Strategic and Defence Studies Centre, The Australian National University, Canberra, 2001.

Unpublished Papers

'A Preoccupation with Armageddon', unpublished memoir, Canberra, 2012.

'Battlefields: New Century, New Norms', unpublished paper, Canberra, 2012.

'China and the Arab Spring', unpublished paper, Canberra, 2012.

'Revolutions and Alliances', unpublished paper, Canberra, 2012.

'The G-20 and Multipolarity', unpublished paper, Canberra, 2012.

www.ingramcontent.com/pod-product-compliance
Lightning Source LLC
Chambersburg PA
CBHW061228270326
41928CB00025B/3446